PROLOGUE

My first 26 years, turned out to be quite an adventure. In 1962, I challenged Lewis & Clark to a race down the 557 miles of Clearwater, Snake and Columbia rivers. They did it in 32 days in canoes and I did it in 27 days swimming. It was done as a publicity stunt to raise money for me to go to college and eventually to medical school. My ambition was to become a researcher in the field of Submarine Medicine. Now, looking back, it seems that after the big river swim, I was starting a new life!

Unfortunately, the feat did not earn me any money and those of you who read my first book, <u>Lewis & Clark and Me</u>, know it was a life changing experience. What I gained from the swim was far more valuable than money. I knew that I could accomplish anything I set as a goal and pursued with my mind, heart, and actions. I learned valuable lessons during my early years. The most important lesson was to take charge of my life and shape my own destiny. I discovered that if your road to success is blocked, there's always a detour. I learned that respect given is almost always given in return.

I found that you could learn from anyone if you have an open mind and you can learn valuable lessons from those whom you might consider your adversaries. I also came to realize that you don't need to rely on degrees and diplomas to obtain and possess knowledge. What my dad once told me is true. He said, "You have the whole world's knowledge at your fingertips when you walk through the doors of a large public Library with the ability to read, reference, and reason." That was my dad's version of the three R's.

I came to understand that certain people in our lives have a profound effect on our attitudes toward success or failure, and it is very important to cultivate relationships with those that create a positive effect. I found that success was not the attainment of an objective, but the continuous journey to obtain other objectives. This wisdom has been stated many times, in many ways by many authors, but we can't fully appreciate its meaning, until we have the experience of successfully reaching a major goal, and realizing that it is only a temporary resting place in a lifelong quest. To those of you who read my first book, <u>Lewis and Clark & Me</u>, thanks for the time and the interest. I hope you will enjoy the episodes of these second 26 years as much as I did living them.

Spence Campbell

ACKNOWLDGEMENTS

To Bill Brubaker for his inspiration and support in writing this book. Elaine O'Neil for her technical assistance on the manuscript and cover design. Drs. John Johnston, Charles Guildner, and Richard Ward for their guidance and support on my original research work. To Dr. Merrill Spencer who believed in my research and gave me my big break. To Dr. Tag Gornall my co-prankster and research buddy. To Rear Admiral Emory Stanley head of the Sea Use program. To Roland White, Vince Rainier, and John Eriksen my Cobb Seamount diving officers. To Commanders Ransome Boyce and Marty Danko our U.S. Coast Guard Ship Captains for many successful Seamount missions. To the Coast Guard crews that supported the Seamount missions. To Chuck Blackstock for the records and films of the Seamount missions. To Kirby Johnson my shark fighting diving buddy. To Bill Aggenbach my ARPA project diving buddy. To Jim Washburn for his support and participation in the Sea Use missions. To Karen Aggenbach for her logistic support for the Seamount Teams. To all the project Sea Use diving teams. To Drs. Bill Postles and Don Callison our submarine medical physicians on the seamount missions. To Sharon Dodge, Sea Use diver and first woman to dive the Cob Seamount. Finally, to my wonderful wife Marie for putting up with me while I wrote the book.

PHOTO CREDITS

To the photographers and organizations that provided pictures and drawings for the book: Virginia Mason Research Center, The Sea Use Program, ESSA, The U.S. Coast Guard.

Photographers: Tag Gornall, Dr. Merrill Spencer, Roland White, Chuck Blackstock, Vince Rainier, and members of the Sea Use Diving Team.

FORWORD

"One way to get the most out of life is to look upon it as an adventure"
- William Feather

I doubt if author-publisher William Feather knew Spence Campbell personally, but I am convinced that he had people like Spence in mind when he penned that quote in his book; The Business of Living.

Spence Campbell's life has been one adventure after another with hardly time to rest in between. No sooner had he dried off from his epic 557-mile swim of three of the world's greatest rivers (Chronicled in his book Lewis And Clark And Me) Spence was at it again, living adventures that would take him from the deserts of the Baja to the depths of the Pacific Ocean. In this highly personal, entertaining and sometimes funny narrative, Spence holds nothing back. the heart aches as well as the rushes of success, and while doing so introduces you to a cast of characters in which he spares nothing in crediting them with much of his own success.

In this account of Spence Campbell's hand over hand climb of the success ladder, you'll share his experiences in training at hospitals to the makeshift laboratory in his garage where his first experiments in diving physiology were conducted, to whale research and the infamous spider shootout in the Baja.

The adventures, it would seem are limitless. Spence Campbell can in a way be likened to Horatio Alger, who wrote about such adventures and Hunter S. Thompson who lived them. <u>After The Swim</u> is a great read and one which you will enjoy and from which you will definitely learn something.

Bill Brubaker, Author of <u>Seamount</u>

CHAPTER 1
GENERAL HOSPITAL

After swimming 557 miles in 27 days, down the Clearwater, Snake, and Columbia Rivers, I realized that I was going to get neither fame nor fortune for the feat. What I did get from the swim was the confidence to set and achieve goals for my life.

With my wife, Susan, and two sons, Ron, and Scott, I moved to Everett, Washington, and took a job as an orderly at Everett General Hospital. I applied, and was accepted into the two-year registered nursing program at Everett Community College. Because I did not have the education or money for pre-med and medical school, I viewed the nursing program as a side door to the medical field. The program would be demanding. I would be working from midnight until 7:30 AM at the hospital and then go to my first class at 8:00 in the morning. Fortunately, the college was only about five blocks from the hospital, and the house that we had rented was about three blocks from the hospital, so at least transportation was not going to be a problem. Susan took a job at a small nearby cafe. She was a hard worker and was great with customers. The cafe owners liked her a lot, and the customers loved her. All our income was used to cover expenses. Every penny went for living or school. Susan never complained. She seemed to have ultimate faith in me and my dreams. As the first academic year progressed, my job at the hospital became more intense. Because of my previous medical training at the state mental hospital in Orofino, Idaho, and my student nursing status, I was given more medical type duties. In addition to working the various floors of the hospital, I worked in central supply and assisted in the emergency room.

The first floor of the hospital consisted of general medical wards and one wing near the main floor nursing station had wards and private rooms for more difficult medical problems, such as drug and alcohol patients. I was the only male on the midnight shift staff except for an E.R. doctor and the occasional practicing physician who stopped by to look in on one of their patients.

During the hundreds of hours of normally routine orderly duties, there were some exciting and unique experiences. Our head nurse on the graveyard shift was a single woman in her mid-thirties. She was tough and demanding, and ruled her shift with an iron hand. When I first started working with her, I got the distinct impression that she didn't like me, or trust me. She was a stern taskmaster and had a very abrasive manner. After we had worked together for several months, she seemed to accept me and took some personal interest in my training as a student nurse. Because of my previous training as a Psychiatric Aide at the Northern Idaho State mental hospital, she was particularly happy to have me on her shift when we had drug and alcohol patients or the occasional psychotic that we had to deal with in a crisis.

I also acquired some specific medical skills from a couple of the urologists that practiced at the hospital. They gave me some special training in catheterization of male patients with urinary problems. After that training, the urologists always specified me to do all their catheterizations. It was an awkward and sometimes embarrassing medical procedure, but someone had to do it. With the number of them that I performed, I acquired a reputation with the medical staff for having expertise in the art of inserting male catheters with a minimal amount of intimidation and pain. Because of post-surgical trauma, there were constant request for this procedure, and the surgical ward always seemed to need my services on the midnight shift.

One night, I arrived at the hospital and the nursing supervisor told me that I was urgently needed on the surgical ward. When I got to the ward, the head nurse, Mrs. Daley, told me that the Dr. had specifically requested me to do a catheterization on a patient that required a large diameter catheter. Mrs. Dailey said that the man was extremely paranoid and intimidated by the procedure. To calm his fears, Mrs. Daley told him that I was an expert at this procedure and that she and the doctor had specifically requested me, because I had done dozens of catheterizations, and all the patients had remarked how surprised they were at how smooth, professional, and painless it was. Apparently, with this glowing endorsement of my skill, the patient was pacified. I thanked Mrs. Daley for her confidence, picked up the Cath tray and headed for the ward.

The patient was the only one in a two-bed ward. He was a heavyset man in his early fifties. He had a pleasant demeanor, and when I introduced myself, he said,

"The nurse told me you are the best. I wouldn't feel a thing, right?"

"I'll try to make it is easy as possible." I said as I drew the isolation drapes around the bed. I put the catheter tray on the bedside stand and started to set up for the procedure. I noticed as I carefully unwrapped the tray that the man was watching my every move. I could tell by the expression on his face that he hadn't completely bought off on the "no pain" endorsement.

Catheterization is a sterile procedure, so after unwrapping the set up. I put on sterile surgical gloves. The equipment required for a catheterization is quite simple. Basically, there are two stainless steel bowls about 7 inches in diameter and four to five inches deep, a pair of surgical gloves, some disinfectant, a medical scissors-like clamp called hemostat, a rubber catheter tube to be installed, and some lubricant to facilitate the installation. Once I put on the surgical gloves, I must maintain a sterile field of work. While I prepared the catheter and the patient, I had to be very careful not to contaminate the sterile field or the catheter.

When I had prepared the sterile field, I opened the package containing the catheter. I carefully peeled down the plastic wrapper, exposing the rubber tube. I extracted the catheter from its packaging with the sterile hemostat. I then put the catheter into one of the stainless-steel bowls. This was a very large diameter catheter, and I tried not to let the patient see it as I transferred it to the bowl, but I think he did, because when I cast a quick glance his way he had that "You're not really putting that in my you know what!" look.

I carefully coiled the large rubber catheter into the bowl, and had just said something encouraging to help him relax when the rubber catheter flexed out of its coil and sprang straight up four feet into the air above the bowl.

I panicked! The sterile field and my careful preparation would be destroyed if the catheter touched anything that was not sterile. The catheter was flying in an arc away from me and was going to drop onto the ward floor beyond the stand. In desperation, I dropped the hemostat and lunged forward, trying to catch the still sterile catheter in my still sterile gloved right hand. The stand was just below waist height, and as I leaned across the stand to save the catheter it began rolling away from me on its wheels. As I leaned into the moving stand, it tipped toward me, and my momentum propelled me over the falling table. There was no stopping! The frantic effort to save the sterile preparation was abandoned for a panic-stricken attempt to save my butt. Too late! I cart wheeled over the stand, grabbing at anything I could to break my fall. The anything became the isolation drapes surrounding the bed.

While in midair, clutching a bunch of drapes in both hands, I was awarded another consequence of wrong choices! The light aluminum railing supporting the drapes didn't come close to supporting my weight. As I held fast to the drapes to break my fall, the railing buckled, bringing down the entire drapery hardware system. I crashed to the floor in a jumble of bedside stand, isolation drapes, and what used to be a sterile catheter set up. One stainless steel bowl went clattering across the ward floor and the other one came to rest right side up, within six inches of my right elbow.

Within a half second the errant, leaping, catheter came out of nowhere and dropped into the bowl (possibly, still sterile.)

I was struggling to get to my feet, when Mrs. Daley appeared in the ward. "What on earth happened?" She cried." Surprised by the wreck I had made. "You won't believe me!" I groaned as I pulled off the drape that was partly wrapped around my head. As I struggled to get to my feet, I suddenly realized that the hardware and back drapes had shrouded the patient's bed, and he was buried beneath a pile of drapery and aluminum hardware. I quickly rushed over and removed the rubble.

"Are you OK?" I asked. He slowly lifted his head; pushed aside the pile of drapes and tubing, then he turned to Mrs. Daley with a bewildered look on his face and said, "Are you sure, he's the best you have?"

After I explained what happened to Mrs. Daley, we stood outside the ward in the hall and laughed until we were exhausted. Afterwards, I went back into the ward, cleaned up the mess, moved the patient to a new bed, and ordered up another catheter set. I then explained my unfortunate mishap to the patient. Upon hearing the whole story of how I destroyed everything, He said, "It sounds hilarious. I wish I could have seen it." Then, both of us laughed ourselves to tears.

Having torn down the last barriers of anxiety along with everything else, I perform his catheterization with my usual finesse, and when it was over, he smiled and said, "Hey, you really are good! Did you hurt yourself when you fell?" "Only my pride." I answered.

I gave the man a "high five" and left the ward to do my nightly duties.

The "Destroyer Catheterization" story was all over the hospital for the next week, and I felt embarrassed until one of the doctors told me how he destroyed an operating room when he was an intern. Someone should write a book on medical personnel induced catastrophes!

Chapter 2
THE GRIND

Maintaining a full-time shift from midnight until 7:30 AM at the hospital and carrying a full-time academic load in the nursing program was more stressful than I anticipated. I enjoyed my classes, especially Anatomy, Physiology, and Microbiology. Unfortunately, the science classes were in the afternoon, and after working all night in the hospital, and attending nursing classes all morning, I had trouble staying awake in the classes I love the best.

I took Physiology, Microbiology, and a Marine biology elective from the same professor, Dr. Thayne Parks. Dr. Parks was the rarest kind of teacher. He knew how to make science fascinating. One day, in Marine Biology, He was teaching us about the Opalescent Nudibranch, an ocean-going version of the common garden variety slug. He explained that this sea slug was beautiful. It had a colored body that was iridescent like the fire opal gem, and that it had an unusual capability.

He said that this Nudibranch fed on the tentacles of the Sea Anemone. This was amazing, because those tentacles contained stinging cells that would paralyze small fish and other small sea creatures that trespassed into them! The stinging cell was a fluid sphere with a coiled barbed spring inside. If disturbed, it would break, stick the intruder, release the toxin, and cause paralysis. The Anemone would then use its tentacles to pass the prey toward its;

gullet and digest it for dinner. Dr. Parks suggested that a non-stinging cell could easily be digested by the Nudibranch, whereas the stinging cell was indigestible. He drew the analogy of a grape compared to a glass marble.

He also suggested that if typical animals ate glass marbles, they would obviously pass them through their system as unwanted waste. He said that the Opalescent Nudibranch was somehow able to keep the stinging cells of the Anemone intact without being stung, and it could pass the cells through its body out on to its brightly colored, short tentacle-like skin to use as a defense mechanism against its predators. He said it was like a human jumping on a bull, eating it whole, and growing horns! He suggested that hidden in the understanding of invertebrate physiology could be the answer to solving tissue rejection in human organ transplants. His lectures were fascinating, and the lesson was always related to the practical world of scientific application.

Despite the large number of students that attended his classes, Dr. Parks seemed to know most of us personally. I once confided to him that I wanted to combine medical science and diving. He thought the idea was unique and went out of his way to encourage and motivate me.

Many times, in his physiology class he caught me nodding off out of sheer exhaustion. He never criticized me for a lack of attention, but one day after the mid quarter, he told me,
"Spence, if you're practicing sleep learning, it's working. You got a 98% on the midterm." Dr. Parks took his place along with my high

school teachers, Marion Shinn, and Maude Adams as educational mentors that helped shape my life.

There was never enough money for family needs, so to make some extra cash I started teaching scuba diving, at the Everett YMCA. In addition to my professional diving credentials, I was a Scuba instructor for the National Association of Underwater Instructors (NAUI) and an Aquatics Director for the YMCA. The extra money that I earned helped a lot. About six months after I started teaching at the YMCA, they lost their gymnastics and fitness instructor and asked me to fill in until they could find a replacement.

With all the extra work, I was finally making a living wage, and Susan and I could afford a few extras. I could even put a little money away in savings. However, the schedule I had worked myself into became a destructive trap! I would attend school from 8 AM until 3:30 PM then go home and sleep until 6:30 PM. I would go to the YMCA and teach until 10 o'clock, and go home and sleep until 11:30. My hospital shift started at midnight, and I would work until 7:30. This regimen continued for months and the only relief I had was an occasional weekend when I wasn't conducting dives in open water in the Puget Sound or teaching classes at the YMCA.

Eventually, the unrealistic pace extracted its toll. It was one night after months of this exhausting schedule that I was at the hospital doing my ward duties. During the beginning of the shift, we had been very busy with a couple of emergency patients and some cleanup work left over by the evening shift.

It was about 3:00 AM. I was making rounds on the ward, taking temperatures and blood pressures when I entered a large five-bed ward. In order, not to disturb all the patients, I left the ward lights off and worked by flashlight or just the dim light coming from the hall through the open ward door. I had just finished picking up a tray of instruments left by the patient's bed and was crossing the middle of the ward toward the door when I looked down and saw huge pile of cotton balls on the floor. *"Who the hell did this?"* I thought to myself, and I began cursing an unknown someone on the evening shift for leaving the mess. I picked up at least a dozen cotton balls, and place them on the tray along with the pans, instruments, and thermometers.

I had just started for the ward door, when I heard a voice whispering my name *"Speeence, Speeence"*. I turned to see which patient was calling, but everyone looked like they were still sleep. I walked back to the darker part of the ward but I couldn't find anyone awake. Again, I started to leave the ward, when I heard the whispering voice again the *"Speeence, Speeence."*

This time, I located the sound, and went over to where a patient was receiving oxygen from a tank next to his bed. The oxygen flowing through the cannula in the patient's nose made a gentle hissing sound, and I figured that it must have been this sound that I had heard, and mistaken for someone whispering my name.

Again, I headed for the ward door when I looked down and saw more cotton balls on the floor. Now, I was ticked off at who it was that made the mess. I bent over, picked up all the cotton balls, and placed them on my tray. Then I walked from the darkened ward out into lighted hallway. As I entered the hallway, I looked down at the tray I was carrying. A wave of disbelief washed over me. There wasn't a single cotton ball in sight!

I stopped dead in my tracks and tried to figure out where they went? I backtracked into the ward. As my eyes adjusted to the semi darkness, I looked down and saw about half a dozen cotton balls lying on the floor at my feet. Somehow, they must have blown off the tray while I was walking across the ward. I picked them up and put them on the tray, this time I covered them with my hand. I walked out into the hall again, but when I lifted my hand from the tray and looked, there were no cotton balls! Oh, Oh, I thought, I must be hallucinating!" I wasn't willing to admit that I was in trouble from stress and sleep deprivation, and despite the unsettling feeling I was having about the hallucinations, I thought I could tough it out until the end of the shift. I would skip classes tomorrow, and get some real rest. Then I would be 'OK'.

Everything seemed to be working smoothly. I didn't see anything weird for the next half-hour, and I thought I would make it to the end of the shift. Fifteen minutes later however, I was coming from another ward where a doctor had performed some minor surgical procedures earlier that evening. I gathered up all the trays and instruments and was carrying them down the hallway toward the nursing station. I must have totally zoned out while walking down the hall because the hall made a 45-degree jog, and I didn't! I was jarred into consciousness the instant I impacted the wall, and realized that I was crashing to the floor with a bunch of pans, trays, and instruments!

The clatter created by the falling equipment brought two of our floor nurses running down the hall to see what had happened. My first instinct was to tell them that I had slipped on a wet spot on the hall floor, but I was so totally disgusted with myself that I just sat there in the rubble, looking down at the floor, shaking my head. When I finally looked up into their concerned and inquiring faces, I uttered a four-letter expletive and said, "Sorry, I'll clean it up." They could tell by my demeanor that interrogating me any further, would be a bad idea!

After I had cleaned up the mess and mopped up the hall, I went straight to the nursing supervisor's office. Mrs. Beaver was sitting at her desk. She looked up from her desk and smiled as I entered the office. "What can I do for you, Mr. Campbell?" She asked. "You can send me home Mrs. Beaver because I'm hallucinating. I am picking up cotton balls that aren't there, hearing voices, and walking into walls. I am incompetent from lack of sleep. I'm afraid I have been pushing myself too hard lately, and trying to do too much with too little sleep."

Mrs. Beaver was a wonderful woman and a great supervisor. She got up from her desk, came over and gave me a big hug. "Go home," She said. "Take tomorrow night off with pay. I was going to award you a paid comp day for all the extra work you've done on your normal days off, and now is a perfect time for it."

As I walked the three and a half blocks to our rented house, I vowed to rearrange my schedule so I wouldn't get into this condition again. When I got home, and got into bed, Susan woke up and I told her what had happened. I told her not to wake me for school. After that, I fell asleep and woke up at four o'clock in the afternoon.

CHAPTER 3
A CHANGE IN DIRECTION

After my experience with extreme fatigue, I did adjust my schedule, to get more rest. The hospital work was great, and I became a valued member of the hospital staff. I was getting decent grades in my science classes, but the nursing program was very time-consuming.

I began to realize that the skills I was developing were going to prepare me for attending to the sick and afflicted, but I wanted medical knowledge specific to my field of interest. I thought seriously about continuing the program, but I decided that my time was too valuable to spend getting a nursing degree.

At the end of the obstetrics quarter, I made up my mind to drop the program, focus on making some money and in my spare time, study academic subjects that would help me understand diving physiology and submarine medicine. The director of the nursing program was a wonderful lady, and she tried to talk me into staying with the program. I told her that I appreciated the opportunity she had given me, but I had made up my mind that my time and energy would be better spent pursuing a science major. Perhaps, later when I had some academic credentials and some money, I would try for medical school.

I stayed working at the hospital for the next six months, and during that time, I became good friends with several of the doctors who taught me about medical procedures that I thought might help me in my studies. With my persistent curiosity and questions, Doctor Bitar, Chief Pathologist at the hospital, took a special interest in me and allowed me to observe and assist him with several autopsies. Once I got over the grim reality of the procedure, I found it to be by far, the most instructive study of anatomy and physiology because it was real, not just colored pictures and diagrams.

I also became good friends with Dr. Charles Guildner an Anesthesiologist at the hospital, who I had taught to Scuba dive. He knew about my intense interest in submarine medicine. Little did I know at that time how important Dr. Guildner's support would be to my future goals.

Early one evening, when I was working swing shift, a patient was brought to the emergency room from small town east of Everett. He had been Scuba diving in a swimming pool and had lost consciousness. When they took him out of the pool, he exhibited stroke-like symptoms. A local doctor diagnosed the patient as suffering from post-traumatic syndrome due to a near drowning episode.

Scuba Diving was a relatively new sport in the early sixties, and most physicians had not received any training in submarine medicine. I was called down to assist in the Emergency Room. When the patient arrived, I heard the story and a description of the symptoms. The young doctor in E.R. was willing to accept the referring doctor's diagnosis and he told the nurse to start a routine admittance.

As a hospital orderly with no medical credentials, I was in a weak position to intervene, but my conscience just wouldn't let me off the hook, so I discreetly suggested to the E.R. doctor that there might be a problem other than a post-traumatic syndrome.

He was a cool, young physician, and he knew that I had been a professional diver. He listened as I explained how a "Cerebral Air Embolism" air bubbles in the brain could have occurred in an eight-foot deep swimming pool. My knowledge of the exact physics and physiology and using correct medical terminology gave my observation a lot of credence.

About 15 minutes before going to the E.R, I had seen Dr. John Johnston, a newly practicing neurosurgeon going into one of the private rooms to visit a patient. I had met Dr. Johnson briefly and remembered that he had been trained by the U.S. navy in submarine medicine. I suggested to the E.R. doctor that Dr. Johnston might be willing to look at the patient and give his opinion. He thought that might be a good idea and he paged Dr. Johnston.

When Dr. Johnston entered the emergency room, we explained the situation and the referring doctor's diagnosis. Dr. Johnston quickly examined the man and then he turned to me "You're right, Spence. I believe he's had an air embolism. Where is the nearest recompression chamber?" He asked. "The nearest treatment facility is the Navy recompression chamber at Keyport over on the Kitsap Peninsula." I replied. "I have an emergency number in my organizer." Dr. Johnston turned to the E.R. doctor.

"It's your call doctor. but if it were me, I would call the Submarine medical physician at Keyport and explain what you have here."

I gave our E.R. doctor the phone number and after a ten-minute conversation with the navy doctor at Keyport, he turned to the nurse and said, "Arrange emergency transportation for this patient to the Navy recompression chamber at Bangor." The patient was transferred and received emergency recompression treatment at the Navy facility. He responded immediately to the treatment and recovered completely without residual effects.

A couple of days later, Dr. Johnston told me that he had received a call from the man and his doctor thanking him for his help. He said he told them that they owed they're thanks to a hospital orderly, who has a background in submarine medicine. The next day, I got calls from the man and his doctor

CHAPTER 4
DR. JOHNSTON

Two weeks after the air embolism incident, Dr. Johnston called me at the hospital and asked me to have lunch with him the next day. I met him at a local restaurant, and we had a great conversation before lunch. We talked about my training and previous experience, then we talked about his goals for his neurosurgical practice and my goal to do diving physiology research.

When lunch was over, he said, "I need a technician to conduct E.E.G.'s and to operate some special test equipment. Are you interested?" I was ecstatic, and said that I was interested. He said, "I'll make a deal. You come to work for me. I'll pay for all your training, gave you a decent salary and flexible hours. I'll support any of your private research, and fund any equipment you might need."

What I was hearing was too good to be true! "You have a deal." I said. "I would consider it a privilege to be your assistant. With your OK, I'll give the hospital a two week notice this afternoon." We shook hands and left the restaurant. I was excited and could hardly wait to tell Susan about the new job and the opportunity. Susan was working that day at her job in the small restaurant, and I stopped by to have some coffee. I told her the exciting news. She was delighted and the rest of our day was a total high! When I gave my notice at the hospital, they didn't want me to go, but all the staff was very happy for me.

The last two weeks of hospital service went far too slow for me. Finally, I reported to Dr. Johnson's office to start my new position. Dr. Johnston introduced me to the office staff, and then set me up for a four- week training program to be able to conduct electroencephalogram tests; recording brain waves for diagnostic purposes. After my training, he allowed me to set my own schedule to give me flexibility with my time. I did all the EEG's by appointment.

Over the next six months, I received training on various neurosurgical testing devices and equipment used in diagnostics and Neurosurgery. One piece of equipment was the "Echo-line," a machine that uses a form of sonar to locate abnormalities in brain size and displacement.

As in the past, I was a regular at the hospital, but now only in daytime, and only to perform tests for Dr. Johnston. Occasionally, if I were up late at night studying, or working on my research project, I would walk over to the hospital for a short, nostalgic visit with Mrs. Beaver and the night shift staff.

Several months passed, and I was getting good at my new job. Dr. Johnston was a unique individual and a terrific Neurosurgeon. His diagnostic skills were outstanding. He had great surgical hands and a great bedside manner. His practice grew by leaps and bounds.

One afternoon, Dr. Johnston called me at the clinic and asked me to go to the hospital to perform an "Echo-line" test on a patient that had suffered a severe blow to the head in a car accident. The "Echo-line" equipment could determine whether the brain had been pushed to one side by the pressure of a large pool of blood between the skull and the tissue covering the brain; it is called a Subdural Hematoma.

I arrived at the hospital and was setting up the equipment for the test when Dr. Johnston appeared, accompanied by eight young nursing students from Providence hospital. He had agreed to take them on his rounds and explain various diagnosis and procedures.

The patient I was preparing for the "Echo line" test was semiconscious, and Dr. Johnston explained the test and what it would show. He said that he had already determined that the patient had a pool of blood on the right side of the head due to the damage tissue on the right side of his head and ear where he had impacted the right window of the car during the accident. He said he was having me conduct the test to prove that a left displacement of the brain centerline would show pressure coming from the pooling blood on the right side. He said by his observations of the patient's trauma and symptoms, he would predict a six-centimeter shift to the left. Before he left the room with the entourage of nursing students, he turned to me and asked me to call him down in x-ray when I had the results.

When I ran the first test, I got a reading that was totally opposite of Dr. Johnson's diagnosis. I hadn't done many "Echo-line" tests so I figured that I might have done something wrong. I reviewed the procedure in the manual. I did not find where I could have made an error so I repeated the test and got the same results.

The test was showing a six-centimeter shift in midline to the right. This was inconsistent with the damage to the right side of the patient's head and face. Dr. Johnston had been dogmatic about his diagnosis, and I wasn't sure how to tell him that we had contrary findings.

To make sure that I was on solid ground with my data, I ran the test very carefully a third time. Same results; there was still a six-centimeter shift to the right. Unless the machine or I were wrong, there was a subdural hematoma pushing against the patient's brain from left side of his head, or the man had an abnormally displaced brain.

I collected tracing photos and walked down to x-ray with the results of the three tests. Dr. Johnston was using some x-ray films of the brain to explain a neurosurgical diagnosis. When I walked into the back of the room, Dr. Johnston saw me and stopped his lecture. Without waiting for me to give him the results of the Echo line test, he said to the student nurses" "Spence is here with the test results that will confirm my diagnosis. What did you find Spence?" All the nursing students turned to look at me with anticipation. Right then, I wanted to be somewhere else! I grimaced slightly, and said. "Doctor you are right on the six-centimeter shift, but all three test I ran show that we have a shift to the right."

Dr. Johnson's face dropped, and for a moment he was speechless. Then his flustered look slowly turned to anger. "The tests are wrong." He said, as he looked at the results. "This can't be," he uttered. "There is no obvious damage to the left less side of his head which would support these findings! Are you positive, the tests were done correctly?"

"I ran three separate tests doctor, and checked my procedure. I'm sure the results are accurate for what the machine is telling us." I replied. "Run one more test, check everything for accuracy." He ordered. "Yes sir." I said, and went back to the patient's floor to do the test again.

I checked everything and carefully ran the fourth test hoping that I might discover some obvious flaw that would reverse the direction of the shift. The results were exactly as before and the photo tracings were identical. I called Dr. Johnston with the results, and after hearing the results, he said "Spence, what do you think?" After a moment of hesitation, I answered. "I think the machine may be right." "I can't buy it." He said. Then there was a long pause on the phone. "Let's prove that the machine isn't correct." He exclaimed. "I'm bringing the patient down for an encephalogram, a test done, which will show an area of pooling blood in the brain. "Come down to x-ray Spence, I want you to see this." Dr. Johnston had this I'm going to prove you and the machine wrong tone in his voice, and I wondered if I might be in trouble?!

Later, Dr. Johnston, the nurses, and I were all in x-ray as a Radiologist brought in the patient's films. He clamped them up on the viewing screen, and he and Dr. Johnston evaluated the x-rays. After a few minutes, Dr. Johnston turned around slowly and faced the nursing students. He looked very solemn and serious.

"Pay close attention to the lesson you are about to learn," he told the students. "I was so sure of my diagnosis that I thought the Echo line test results couldn't possibly be right. I even thought that Mr. Campbell might not have conducted the test properly. "Spence, you have my apologies. The x-ray test identifies a large hematoma on the left side, creating a six-centimeter right shift exactly as shown by the "Echo line" tests."

Dr. Johnston then turned to the x-rays explaining the technical side of the findings. After the explanation was finished, he looked at the students and said. "Don't ever allow yourself to become so self-righteous in your medical judgment that you don't need a backup test or a second opinion. I was willing to delay surgery based on my original diagnosis, but due to Mr. Campbell's test results, and his refusal to capitulate on the validity of those results, we are going to surgery tomorrow morning. I will arrange an observation Gallery for those of you who are able to attend."

I was amazed that Dr. Johnston was so open about the missed diagnosis, but that's the way he was, honest and direct. He wanted those nursing students to know that no one is above reproach, and that a good medical professional does the extra things required to confirm the validity of the diagnosis and treatment.

In the morning, I arrived at Providence hospital at 6 AM to "scrub in" with Dr. Johnston for the surgery. When I entered the operating room, I saw about eleven nursing students seated in the observation Gallery. Dr. Johnston began the surgery, and he allowed me to assist him. The pressure area was exactly where the test indicated and when the pressure had been successfully relieved, Dr. Johnston looked up at the Gallery, gestured toward me and said, "If we had delayed the surgery this patient may have died or never recovered properly. Thanks to Mr. Campbell, he will be fine now." The Gallery applauded, and I was overwhelmed!

During our lifetimes, we all incur our share of misdiagnosis and "bone-head" mistakes, but every so often you find yourself a winner. Dr. Johnston was one of a kind, because he was as demanding of himself as he was of others. He was a great doctor and a great friend. I will never forget the lessons he taught and the encouragement and help that he gave to me.

CHAPTER 5
BATHROOM SCIENCE

I spent most of my off-duty time searching the scientific literature and studying all the research work completed about decompression sickness, known as *"the bends"*. I was fascinated by the challenge of what caused divers to get the bends, and how it might be prevented. At that time, prevention was accomplished basically by having the divers ascend slowly and remain at various shallow depths for enough time to let nitrogen gas compressed into the tissues during the dive to escape slowly. In my quest for information on the subject, I even obtained research papers in German, French, Russian, and Norwegian. I had them translated so that I could see what scientists in other countries had discovered.

Decompression sickness was a constant threat for divers going to deep depths or staying for long periods of time at shallow depths. A series of decompression tables had been developed by the naval research groups of several countries. These tables were used in the field with reasonable success, but they were not 100 percent foolproof, and divers still suffered some decompression sickness problems while using the tables. Sometimes these divers would manifest lesser symptoms of "the bends," which ranged from discrete tingling sensations to acute pain. More serious problems would be stroke and cardiac arrest.

As I studied and understood more about the problem, I was fascinated by the complexity of the factors contributing to the cause of decompression sickness. Because of the way my mind functioned, and my shortcoming in mathematics, I was forced into a relatively unsophisticated and simplistic approach to the problem. After I had studied all the subject matter I could find, I spent a few days asking myself questions for which I had no answers.

I had a better background in mechanics than in medical science, so I perceived the initial problem to be like that of a plugged-up toilet. Too much nitrogen gas was trapped inside the body, causing pressure and destroying sensitive tissue. The normal path to get nitrogen out of the body and blood was through the lungs, but during "the bends," nitrogen gas was expanding within the divers' blood and other tissues. This created bubbles, and an unwanted kind of sludge in the blood. This sludge would plug up the lungs and wouldn't let the nitrogen escape properly.

Since I was using the, *"plugged toilet"* approach, I knew that one way to clear a toilet was to use force. A plunger solves this problem most of the time when used on a toilet. Other researchers had already discovered that having the divers breathe pure oxygen, there would be no nitrogen partial pressure in the lungs to cause resistance. The result would be the same as having more push to get nitrogen out of the system.

Oxygen had been shown to be effective. To some degree, the "plunger" solution was working, but not effectively enough to prevent "the bends" all the time. Oxygen also has its drawbacks.

Breathing pure oxygen underwater at a depth of 33 feet could make it toxic to the system, producing a convulsive-like reaction causing the diver to drown

Another way to clear a plugged toilet is to pour a lot of water into the bowl, making more room for the clogging stuff to spread out and get through the pipes. This also provides a certain amount pressure because of the added weight of the water. Researchers had already suggested injecting compatible fluids into the blood to accomplish much the same thing. These fluids are called plasma expanders.

Additionally, you can clear a plugged toilet by thinning out the clogging substances. Two Canadian researchers studied the clogging substances that cause the blood to create sludge. Because gas bubbles form in the blood during the ascent after a significant dive, the blood near the bubbles tends to coagulate as blood does when it oozes from a cut and contacts air. One of the reasons for blood to form sludge was due to "platelet aggregation" meaning that blood particles begin to group and stick together in a clump.

These researchers also found that oils from damage fat cells leak a type of oil called "lipoprotein" into the blood stream, which forms a coating around the bubbles present in the blood, like the soap bubbles that you blew when you were a kid. This oil coating around the bubble clogs up the lungs, making it difficult for the gas to escape from the body during decompression.

The Canadian researchers used a blood thinning medication to help prevent blood coagulation, and a chemical, that dissolves fatty oils. They found that both substances helped with the clogging problem.

After studying all the current treatment research, I realized that there was one aspect of a plugged toilet that hadn't been addressed. If there were some way to make the toilet discharge pipes larger, the clogging would have less resistance and would pass through the opening easier. There are small pipes or blood vessels in the lungs that might be enlarged, which would help reduce the problem. The chemical that could produce this effect is called a vasodilator. I reasoned that exploring this possibility was worth a series of experiments. As Sherlock Holmes, would put it, "the game was afoot!"

First, I would need a "decompression chamber," a steel cylinder capable of holding air pressure that could simulate a depth of 200 feet of sea water. A close friend of mine, Chuck Griswold, who was also a diving instructor, donated a chamber that had been fabricated from a low-pressure compressed air tank. It had one port that allowed you to observe inside the tank, and a hatch that could be sealed and bolted. With some work and minor modification, it would be suitable for the experiments.

Next, I would need some materials to build special equipment that would hold small test animals and a delivery system for the medications I wanted to test. I shared my hypothesis with Dr. Johnston who thought it had merit. He encouraged me to build the equipment and conduct the tests. He also made a cash donation to help fund the research.

Armed only with intuition, self-education, and naive enthusiasm, I started my initial experiments. It took about two months to fabricate the apparatus I needed to conduct the series of tests. I used a variety of items from a local hardware store. These items which included a large plastic cake cover were hardly identifiable as medical research equipment and I got a strange look from Susan when she saw what I bought home. After working at the clinic and the hospital, I would spend most nights until 2:00 or 3:00 AM building a small laboratory in the basement of our rented house. Susan would bring down late-night snacks for me, and would try to get some insight into what on earth her crazy husband was doing in their basement. She would ask me questions, and I would try to explain the project to her.

One night, after trying to explain a technical concept to her, she looked at me, and with a straight face, asked, "These experiments don't involve bringing high-voltage electricity from lightning bolts into the basement, do they?" I chuckled at her jibe, "Yes," I quipped. "Would you like to see the body I've sewn together? It's in the freezer!" We both broke up laughing, and then she went back upstairs to bed as I continued working on my apparatus.

Susan was a great sport about me spending so much time on the project. she seemed to understand how important the research might be. She was so supportive and patient, I felt guilty about not spending as much time as I should with her and my two small sons.

I finally finished building all the experimental equipment. I was now ready to start tests. My guinea pigs would be real guinea pigs, and I conducted a few preliminary experiments to get some baseline data. I had to make some adjustments after my first series of tests, but the results I got from my second set of tests were very encouraging. After a couple of months, the experiments were going well. I was very excited about the results.

One weekend, I was visiting some friends that own a sport Scuba Diving shop in Bellevue, Washington. They wanted me to teach their Scuba diving classes. I wanted to keep up my diving skills so I agreed to teach the evening classes. Over the next few months, I drove back and forth from Everett to Bellevue two nights a week for the diving classes. I also drove from Everett to Seattle on another two nights to attend a course in Human Factors Engineering at the University of Washington. Traveling 30 miles back to Everett late at night after the classes got old in a hurry! After a couple of months of it, I figured it would be easier to live in Bellevue and commute to Everett for work each day, and be close to home after night school and evening diving classes.

Susan and I found a small three-bedroom house that was located near a new hospital right in the middle of Bellevue. It was about 10 minutes from the Skin Diver's Cove dive shop, and about fifteen minutes across Lake Washington to the University. It took about a month to finalize the purchase of the house and complete the move from Everett to Bellevue. Susan was elated with the idea of owning our own home. The house had a carport and a garage, and while Susan was setting up and furnishing the house, I turned the garage into a laboratory for my research work. Once everything was set up and functioning in the lab, and I got used to the change in daily routine, I resumed my experiments.

One day, when I was doing a test for Dr. Johnston at Everett General hospital when I ran into, Dr. Guildner, the anesthesiologist. Dr. Guildner had been a student in one of my SCUBA diving classes at the YMCA. I got to know him quite well and we had discussed my research work and the results of my recent experiments

Dr. Guildner said that one of his medical school professors, Dr. Richard Ward was an associate professor at the University of Washington Medical School in the Department of Anesthesiology. He said Dr. Ward would be very interested in the research work I was doing, and asked if he could contact him concerning my work. I told him that I would be happy to talk with Dr. Ward and show him what was I was doing.

It was about three weeks after talking with Dr. Guilder that I received a call from Dr. Ward inquiring about the research. I invited him to visit my makeshift garage laboratory in Bellevue to see what I was doing. The next Tuesday evening Dr. Ward came to my home in Bellevue. I had prepared a demonstration experiment so he could see the equipment and protocol I was using, and judge the results. When the session was over, he turned to me and said, "Spence, what you're doing here is valid research, and with some refinement, you have results worthy of a paper in the medical literature." He offered to assist me in developing a proper scientific protocol, and said we could do the experiments under the University's mantle.

I couldn't believe my ears and was very excited. In the next few weeks, I signed a document collaborating with Dr. Ward and the University. My garage laboratory had a sticker on the hot-water heater that proclaimed my garage laboratory as an annex research facility of the University of Washington Medical School. Dr. Ward brought over some supplies and medications needed for the new series of experiments, and the scientific protocol for us to follow. During the next month, we conducted all the experiments called for in the plan. The research findings proved to be significant enough for a formal paper. Dr. Ward presented that paper at the American Society of Anesthesiologists Conference in Salt Lake City.

The paper, titled, *Experimental Prevention of Decompression Sickness* by S. D. Campbell, and R. J. Ward, was printed in the "American Journal of Anesthesiology" January/ February 1969

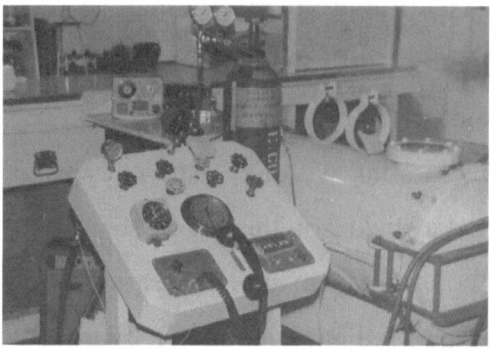

My garage laboratory in Bellevue

Article in the Seattle paper on starting the Diving Physiology Laboratory at the Virginia Mason Research Center.

Initial laboratory equipment, moved to the research center from my garage in Bellevue.

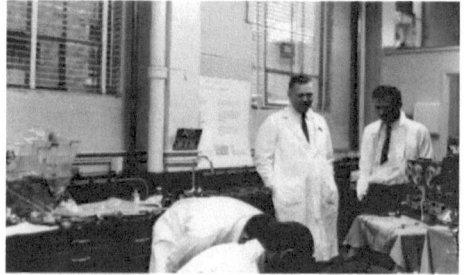

Dr. Merrill Spencer, John Linbergh and two of my laboratory interns preparing for a decompression experiment.

CHAPTER 6
DR. SPENCER AND VMRC

Susan had her hands full with our two small sons, Ron and Scott, and she was having some medical complications from her diabetes. The long commute from Bellevue to Everett each day was stressful and with teaching scuba classes and attending classes at the university, I didn't have much family life. Still consumed with enthusiasm for the research, I started another series of experiments exploring a different aspect of the problem of preventing severe decompression sickness.

At that time, one of the people taking my Scuba Diving course was Bill Brubaker. Bill was the news anchor on KOMO.TV in Seattle. He was interested in the work I was doing and he produced and narrated a 20-minute documentary film on my research that was shown on Channel 4 in Seattle.

The day after the documentary aired, I received a call from Dr. Merrill Spencer. Dr. Spencer was the Director of the Virginia Mason Research Center in Seattle. He had seen the program and wanted to come and talk with me. The next night, he came to my home and we had an inspiring meeting. He said he was impressed with my current research work and that he was thinking about developing a department at the center for diving physiology research. The Center currently had several research departments involved in a variety of medical studies. They were doing Kidney research, Anesthesia research, and Dr. Spencer's own research work in blood flow and the diving reflex of marine mammals.

Dr. Spencer's studies led him to become very interested in the respiratory and blood flow physiology of Marine mammals and human divers. Marine mammals are air breathers like humans, but they can dive to extreme depths and stay submerged for long periods of time. The Elephant Seal has recorded dives deeper than 1000 feet, and can stay submerged for over 30 minutes. The average human would be uncomfortable after being submerged to a depth of 10 or 15 ft. and holding their breath for much over 30 seconds.

There are reasons that some marine mammals can perform deep dives for long periods of time. Marine mammals have a respiratory and blood vascular system that is designed to allow these kinds of dives. They also possess a remarkable diving reflex that slows all their bodies' metabolic functions and keeps them from needing air or suffering ill effects from not breathing for prolonged periods.

Remnants of this diving reflex are rooted in the history of human physiology. There are a small number of human divers that can perform "breath hold" dives routinely to depths of over 100 feet for times of over four minutes without suffering ill effects. A human diver has gone deeper than five hundred feet on a "breath hold" dive. At shallower depths, these divers might occasionally make underwater times of up to five minutes or more.

All humans have a diving reflex to some degree. In my fifties, I conducted a seminar called "Secrets of the Diving Reflex." I taught hundreds of sports scuba divers how to develop their diving reflex. In a two-day training seminar, I could take groups of divers who could average only around 30 seconds underwater at a depth of 10 or 12 feet and improve their ability to stay comfortably submerged for up to two minutes. When I trained them in warm, clear tropical, open water they could make dives to 50 feet for two or more minutes.

The work Dr. Spencer was doing was fascinating to me and we talked for some time about potential joint research projects. Dr. Spencer said he would like to keep in touch with me on my research and I thanked him for his interest. To have someone with Dr. Spencer's standing and reputation interested in my research was fulfilling. After he left, I was excited and greatly encouraged.

Several days after Dr. Spencer's visit, Susan gave me a message that Dr. Spencer wanted me to call him at his home that evening. When I called, he said, "Spence. I'm glad you called. I've been thinking about your work and the direction I want to go with my work. I believe you and I can work together to develop a Diving Physiology Research Department at Virginia Mason Research Center. Would you be interested in continuing your work at VMRC and managing the new laboratory?"

The impact of his query was like an electric jolt! Dr. Spencer was offering me a job in diving research with the most prestigious medical research Center in the Northwest. My mind was playing ping-pong with my emotions! Suddenly, a terrible thought crossed my mind. I had never discussed my academic background with Dr.

Spencer. He may think that I have academic credentials. At that moment, I felt education-poor as I had little to offer.

"Dr. Spencer," I said. "My life's major goal would be fulfilled if I could accept your offer, but I have to tell you that I don't even have a baccalaureate degree." There was a long moment of tense silence as I waited for his response, and I could feel my dream job dissolving into a misfortunate fantasy!
"Spence." He said. I've had dozens of people with master's degrees and Ph.D.'s working with me and they did nothing. You're doing something significant. I like your approach to research, and you don't need any degrees to come and work with me." I was in shock. "I'll need a reasonable time to help Dr. Johnston train another technician," I said. "Plan to start the first of next month". Dr. Spencer replied. "That should give you an adequate time to make your transition. Welcome to the VMRC team. Call me if you have any concerns or questions".

After hanging up the phone, I stood silently for several minutes. I was experiencing a feeling of overwhelming joy and giddy excitement that I hadn't felt since I was a child anticipating some special treat. Immediately, I went to the kitchen to find Susan. She was standing at the kitchen counter fixing diner. I took her by the shoulders and turned her to face me "If I drank champagne, and you drank at all, I would go get a bottle, so we could celebrate." I said, trying to play it cool. "What would we celebrate?" She asked, rather surprised by my statement. "I now have a new position as manager of the diving physiology laboratory at Virginia Mason

Research Center." I announced. "What!" She exclaimed. "When did this happen?" "The phone call to Dr. Spencer, he offered me the position, and I accepted." Now, I let all the pent-up excitement show as I offered Susan a high five. Oh, Spence! I'm so happy for you." She replied as she threw her arms around me for a big hug and kiss.

Then, as a practical, down to earth thinking wife would do, she asked, "What did he offer you for a salary?" "Salary?" I responded, as my naïve enthusiasm ground slowly to a halt. "He never said anything about a salary, and I never asked." I said." "Spence," she said, her voice soft but firm. "I know that this is an answer to your dreams, and you would probably do it for free, but you have a family, and you need to negotiate a good wage."

Of course, Susan was right, I would have done it for free, but I did need a living wage. Over the next few days, Dr. Spencer and I settled on decent compensation. Now, both Susan, and I were excited about the future.

The next day, I told Dr. Johnston about the offer. Dr. Johnston didn't want me to leave, but he said I would be foolish not to take advantage of such an opportunity. Over the next few weeks, we found another technician, and I did as much training as I could until I left at the end of the month.

In the four days, I took off, before I started at Virginia Mason Research Center, I spent time with Susan and our two sons. There was a new feeling about life. The intense drive to achieve was satisfied for the moment. I thoroughly enjoyed those days. I was excited to begin Diving Physiology Research as a professional, validated by Virginia Mason Research Center. At this point, some of you adventure lovers might be picturing a medical laboratory with a lot of mundane, boring science. Well, hang on to your hat! My new job would prove to be anything but mundane or boring!

When I reported for work that first Monday, I was met by Dr. Spencer and introduced to the administration staff. I spent the rest of the morning, processing into the system, and touring the facility. I met the head of the various research groups, and was introduced to three members of the Board of Directors. After lunch, Dr. Spencer and I examined a large empty space in the building, and made some plans for future development of a diving physiology laboratory.

Dr. Spencer was a consummate researcher, and his enthusiasm for new discoveries and new knowledge was infectious. We talked for a couple of hours about future plans for the laboratory and research projects. We both got very excited about the potential of a new Diving Physiology research laboratory. The last part of the afternoon was getting to know the technicians and scientist who would support us in the research work.

After the first two weeks at VMRC, Dr. Spencer came into the lab and handed me a white lab coat, and a nametag with my name and title. By this time, I had moved the chamber and all the experimental equipment from my garage into the lab at the research Center.

The first order of business was to write a proposal for a research grant to support the lab and our experiments. I had zero experience at writing a research proposal, but Dr. Spencer was a past member of the grant review board at the National Institutes of Health and he knew exactly how a proposal should be prepared. I thought perhaps he would just write the proposal, but I was wrong. One morning, he put a pile of papers containing grant-writing criteria on my desk. He said to read the requirements, study the format, and consult him about anything I didn't understand. Then he added, "When you feel like you have a handle on it, write the proposal." "But, I don't know how to write such an important document!" I confessed. "You'll learn." He said. That was my indoctrination into the realm of grant proposal writing.

Over next four years, I would write several proposals and scientific papers for research. Dr. Spencer would be my mentor, and nemesis, throughout each proposal and article. I would soon write and re-write each paper numerous times. Dr. Spencer was a merciless critic of written documents. Just when I thought I had it perfect, he would change something and have me do it over again.

One day, Dr. Spencer's wife, Jean, came to the research Center. She was looking for Dr. Spencer and came into the diving physiology lab and found me in my office, busy writing a research article for the ninth time. She was looking for Dr. Spencer, but she noticed the manuscript spread out over my desk with Dr. Spencer's red notes and corrections. "Re-writing a paper for Merrill?" She asked. "Yes mam," I answered. "I find that I have to work a lot to get it right for Dr. Spencer." She flashed an all-knowing grin. "Spence," she said. "If it's any consolation, one of Dr. Spencer's closest colleagues once remarked that if you handed Merrill the 23rd

Psalm, he would hand it back with corrections!" We both laughed, and I felt some relief from the pressure of the intense rewriting chore.

I did write my articles and proposals over many times, but I was learning more with each rewrite. In a strange way, I didn't mind. I considered it as technical writing training. I knew that Dr. Spencer's experience on the grant review committee qualified him to know exactly what it took to get a proposal accepted by NIH, and I was rewarded when they were accepted. I became the principal investigator on two NIH grants for Diving Physiology research.

CHAPTER 7
THREE GRINGOS

It was fall in Seattle, and I had been at the research center for about five months. I was developing a new research plan to test another theory I had for preventing severe decompression sickness. One morning, Dr. Spencer came into the lab and asked me to be part of his team on a scientific expedition to study Grey Whales in Baja, Mexico. The National Geographic Society would be sponsoring the expedition. Dr. Spencer wanted me to act as the Chief Diver on the expedition. I was excited and accepted the offer immediately. The thought of getting to dive with the grey whales on a National Geographic Expedition was exhilarating!

During the next few months, we had several planning meetings with other expedition team members, and we developed and tested equipment that would be used to study the whales. The operations would be conducted in Scammon's Lagoon, Baja California, Mexico; an area made famous from early whaling days. Our expedition camp would be located on the beach at Laguna Ojo De Liebre, the "*Eye of The Rabbit Lagoon.*" The purpose of the expedition was to study the respiratory physiology and diving habits of the Grey Whale.

Scammon's Lagoon, a nursery for newly born whale calves is a series of narrow channels that vary from about 10 feet to 50 feet in depth. Mother Grey whales use these shallow channels to give birth to their babies and teach them how to swim and breathe after birth. When the calves get strong enough, and they can keep up with their mother, she takes them out of the protective waters of the lagoon into the open ocean.

One month before we were scheduled to leave on the expedition, I read some information on the area and about the small town of Guerrero Negro. It was the site of a large salt exporting company; the town is located on the Pacific coast near the boundary between North and South Baja. The area consists mostly of ocean beach and desert. The whaling lagoons are about 15 miles south of the town.

While I was planning what to pack for the upcoming expedition, I got the bright idea to take my 9 shot 22-caliber pistol and a bunch of ammunition. Someone told me that there were lots of ducks on the beaches of the lagoons, so I took several boxes of 22-caliber bird shot shells. I had a nice fast draw holster and ammo-belt with a large ornate western buckle. It looked like something out of an old cowboy movie. In addition to my personal stuff and clothing, I packed a couple of medical textbooks I wanted to study.

There was a lot of preparation for the expedition, and we amassed a lot of equipment. Most of the equipment and supplies were loaded aboard a cargo ship that transported salt from Guerrero Negro to Seattle. The ship would sail back to Mexico with our gear about three weeks before we were to leave. The expedition equipment and supplies would be kept in the salt companies' large warehouse until we arrived.

The Expedition supplies included enough lumber to build a small two- room headquarters building that would serve as our Kitchen/dining area and a small lab room for our scientific test equipment. It also included a pick-up truck, two small boats, and a two-man helicopter that would be used to get us in position to tranquillize one of the whales. The objective was to tranquillize one of the whales, herd it up a lagoon into shallow water with the boats, and make scientific measurements and tests on the stranded whale before the tranquillizer wore off and the incoming tide floated the animal.

Tag Gornall, Leonard Lockett, and I would make up the advanced crew. It would be our job to get all the equipment to the expedition site, set up the camp, and scout the area for our operations. Tag, was a research biologist at Virginia Mason Research Center, working with Dr. Spencer on marine mammal research. Leonard Lockett was an excellent carpenter and mechanic, and he took care of all the animals used in studies at the research center. Leonard would build our expedition headquarters shack and serve as our cook and camp manager for the expedition.

Initially, Tag, and I would be responsible to get all the expedition equipment out to camp and help Leonard with the headquarters project. When camp was organized, we would launch the Boston Whaler boat and do some preliminary scouting of the lagoon channels near our campsite.

Finally, the time came to start the expedition. Tag, Leonard and I flew to San Diego by commercial airline and took a cab to Tijuana, Mexico. At the Tijuana airport, we boarded an old DC –3 twin-engine aircraft, owned and operated by the salt company to transport cargo and personnel to and from their plant location in Guerrero Negro.

The contrast between the commercial jet we took from Seattle and the appearance of the aging and well-used cargo plane was worthy of comment. It wouldn't get points for comfort either, as the accommodation was basically metal bench seating. It was functional, however, and about the only way to get to Guerrero Negro.

The flight from Tijuana took about two hours. It was about 6:30 PM when we finally rumbled to a stop on a dirt and gravel strip just outside the town. It was February (winter for us Seattleites), but here, midway down the Gulf of California, it was summer to us. Immediately, both Tag and I realized that we were dressed far too warm for this climate.

When we arrived, we expected to be met by a representative from the Mexican government. He was a marine biologist who was supposed to be our liaison and interpreter, but when we got off the plane, there were just a few Mexican workers who were there to off-load cargo from another plane that was parked alongside the runway.

After the workers finished unloading the planes, they disappeared from the runway. Only two workers were left with the cart and cargo from our plane. Once the last crate was offloaded, the pilots boarded the planes, waved at us from the cockpit window and with a lot of dust and noise, taxied the aircraft to the end of the gravel strip and took off on their return flights. We were totally at a loss as for what to do next, as we watched the planes disappear in the distance. When the dust had settled and it was all too quiet, we looked around at each other and realized that the only thing left at Guerrero Negro Airport were three gringos and three suitcases!

The last two workers that had been off-loading the DC-3 were now pushing their cargo cart down the road toward a large metal building. Tag hollered to them and they stopped and waited for us to catch up. We asked them where we could go to find someone who knew we were coming. They were very polite and smiled all the while we were talking. When we were finished, they just shrugged their shoulders. It was obvious that neither one of them spoke any English. Now, I understood what it felt like to be a foreigner, and I realized that if any communication were going to occur here it would be in Spanish!

Tag said he taken Spanish in school, but couldn't remember anything except how to say hello and ask for a beer. Leonard was restricted to the word "si," and it became painfully obvious to me that the burden of trying to communicate was going to fall on me.

I hadn't taken any formal Spanish in school, but I had driven a truck in the pea harvest for a summer job when I was in high school. I drove a truck that transported peas on the vine from the field where they were cut, to the Viners, machines that strip the peas from the vine. When you reach the Viners, you dump the peas on the ground in front of the machine, and Mexican laborers would use pitchforks to load the peas into the Viners.

My work shift was from 7 PM to 7 AM. At midnight, we had an hour for lunch. During my lunch break, I would park the truck by the Viners, sit with the Mexican workers and try to learn some Spanish. I would point to something and say it in English and then they would say it in Spanish. In the two and a half months that I worked in the pea harvest, I learned quite a few Spanish words, but I didn't know how to make sentences. I knew that if someone ever spoke to me in Spanish it would be a one-sided conversation.

Later, when I was in the Air Force, I bought a recorded course in Spanish and learn some fundamental sentence structure. My total Spanish vocabulary possibly consisted of a couple hundred words because I had learned that any English word ending with the letters "TION" was probably a Spanish word as well. I knew that my attempt to speak Spanish to anyone here was going to be both humorous and painful.

After the two Mexican workers left us, we tried to figure out what to do. So, we picked up our luggage and followed them to the large metal building about a quarter of a mile from the airstrip. It was the only building in sight that looked like a warehouse that could be housing our expedition supplies.

When we got to the metal building, the door was open. As we entered, we could see that it was the main company warehouse. We looked around and saw the helicopter, boat, and pickup along with pallets of our expedition equipment and supplies sitting in one corner of the building. We all breathed a sigh of relief, knowing at least we were in the right town!

There was an office with a counter around it in the center of the building. When we approached, we found an older gentleman doing some paperwork. In my poor Spanish, I asked him if he spoke English. He said he only knew a few words. Unfortunately, *"hello"* and *"where is the toilet?"* wasn't much help. In my best, poor Spanish, I introduced myself and then Tag and Leonard. I apologize for my language shortcomings and asked him to please speak slowly. He was very polite, and extremely empathetic with my attempts to communicate in Spanish.

After some discussion, which included drawings, hand signs, and anything else I could use to get my thoughts and questions across, I determined that his name was Miguel and that he had been expecting us. He said that we could take the expedition equipment whenever we wanted it. I also found out that there were no hotels or restaurants. Miguel said, because we had no camp yet, we were welcome to stay in the warehouse for the night.

When Leonard learned that we were free to access the expedition equipment, he located three cots, three sleeping bags, a small propane camp stove, and some canned soup and crackers. Leonard cooked up some soup and we all had a cup. It was the best soup I ever tasted because I hadn't eaten anything since breakfast! After our impromptu supper, we sat around on the cots and planned our move to the eye of the rabbit lagoon. We had a map of the town and the road leading to the expedition site, which was marked on the map.

As we talked, it grew dark outside. About 10:00 PM Miguel came to tell us that he had to leave and lock up the warehouse. He said he had to turn off the lights. Leonard had retrieved some of our camping lanterns and we told Miguel we would all be fine until morning. He showed us where the toilet and wash basin were located and pointed to a button on the central desk. He said it would ring a buzzer in his trailer just outside the warehouse as he was also the night watchman. Miguel said to call if we had a problem or needed him. We thanked him for his help and consideration and I could do that with some degree of competence because consideration ends in "TION." It wasn't long after Miguel left that the warehouse was plunged into darkness. We sat talking in the lantern light for a few minutes. Then we turned out the lanterns and tried to get some sleep.

It was hot earlier in the evening, but as night fell, the temperature dropped. By late evening it got very cool. About 1:00 AM we were all awakened to what sounded like an animal scurrying around inside the warehouse making strange sounds. About twenty minutes later, we heard something large flying back and forth over our sleeping area. Whatever it was made several low passes over our bunks and it was quite annoying and spooky. Imaginations can run a little wild in the dark and none of us were inclined to turn on the light to see what it was, lest the Seattle newspapers might have read

THREE SEATTLE EXPEDITION MEMBERS KILLED BY GIANT VAMPIRE BAT IN SMALL MEXICAN TOWN!

After several minutes, whatever it was, finally landed somewhere and we all drifted off to sleep again.

In the morning, we asked Miguel what the big thing that that we heard flying around during the night might be? He looked very concerned and gave us an answer in Spanish that none of us understood. We all just nodded our heads and acted unconcerned about it since we were not going to be spending anymore nights in the warehouse.

TAG GORNALL, LEONARD AND SPENCE ARRIVE ON THE DC-3

LAGUNA OJO DE LEIBRE
EYE OF THE RABBIT LAGOON.

SALT TRUCKS LOADING AT THE SALT PONDS.

ROAD FROM THE SALT PONDS TO THE TOWN. DOMAIN OF THE "STRAIGHT ROAD DRIVERS."

OFFSHORE FROM THE LAGOON WE SAW MANY WHALES JUMPING. THESE JUMPS ARE CALLED "SPY HOPS" WHERE THE WHALE CAN GET A LOOK AROUND.

CHAPTER 8
STRAIGHT ROAD DRIVERS

Some workers came into the warehouse about 6 AM we got up and dressed into shorts and light-weight shirts. It was still quite cool, but the morning sun was rapidly warming up the metal building, making the temperature comfortable. I found Miguel and asked him if there was somewhere to get breakfast. He said there was a Cantina on one of the streets of the small town and that they might be able to fix us something when they opened.

Some of the warehouse workers helped us to clear an area around the expedition pickup so we could drive it out of the warehouse. Now at least, we had some transportation. The center of town was only about a half mile down the road. The town itself was very small with some modest houses provided by the Company for the more affluent employees, possibly managers and foremen. The rest of the town, except for a few stores and a Cantina, consisted of several small shacks.

On one end of town, there were some shacks made entirely of cardboard. There were families with several small children living in those cardboard and dirt dwellings. Realizing how poor these people were in material things, changed my prior concept of the term "poor." I started feeling guilty for the bounty that I had and previously considered below average. I mentioned my feelings to Tag and he said he was having the same reaction. Leonard had spent

some time in very impoverished, foreign countries, and he said that people lived and existed in conditions far worse than these.
The Cantina opened at eight o'clock, and the owner made us a breakfast of eggs and pork sausage. Several Mexican men came into the Cantina and they kept staring at us while we ate. It was obvious that new people in town was a rarity.

After breakfast, we returned to the warehouse and hitched the boat trailer to the truck. Then we packed as much camping gear as possible into the pickup and loaded some foundation lumber, tools, and a generator into the boat. We got some directions from Miguel on how to find our campsite, and a warning to look out for the salt trucks! With the aid of his directions and our map, we stated down the only road south to the Eye of the rabbit lagoon.

During the drive, we kept a lookout for the huge salt trucks with big trailers that were hauling loads of salt from the evaporating ponds to the processing plant. The road was primitive and barely wide enough for the big trucks. We had only traveled about three miles before we met the first huge salt truck coming down the road at high speed. We moved our pick-up as far to the side of the road as possible with only two wheels on the road. We expected that the big truck would move over to the opposite side for us, but instead, it stayed right in the middle of the road. We had to take an abrupt detour through the sagebrush to avoid being hit! As we slid to a complete stop in a cloud of sand, and dust, the big truck roared by with a very intense looking driver behind the wheel. "Wow!" Leonard exclaimed. "That was close. That guy never gave an inch."

"Yea, guess they own the road down here." Tag added. It was only about six miles farther down the road, when we were run off the road again by another salt truck! It was plain to see that they were not going to give any quarter. That probably explained all the tire tracks running parallel to the road out in the desert.

We arrived at the campsite lagoon and found a primitive side road that led from the main road to the beach near a small peninsula. A sandy beach tapered gently down to the edge of the water of the lagoon. To the West and South, there was a vast expanse of water channels that make up Scammon's Lagoon. East and north of the peninsula, the beach area was only about 15 to 20 yards wide, and there was an abrupt 3 to 4-foot rise from the beach onto the desert. The sand at the water's edge was grey, and it stretched from the water to hard, sun baked mud at the edge of the desert.

The desert to the east of the lagoon was flat, tapering up to far-off hills that were some miles in the distance. The desert land was sandy with mesquite, sagebrush, and rocks, and it was alive with a variety of life. Birds of various kinds flew about the beaches. The wild life was plentiful and interesting to watch, but the poisonous snakes, scorpions, and spiders that inhabited the area were of most concern to us!

The water was relatively clear. It was not cold, but it was cool to the touch. We stood for a period and stared out into the channel. It wasn't long before we saw our first whales. They were out in mid-channel and they put on a show by executing a few "*spy hops*" where they pop up half way out of the water to look around.

Sighting the whales was exciting and it stimulated our enthusiasm for the expedition.

We unhitched the boat trailer and unloaded the lumber, tools, and generator that Leonard needed to start building our main headquarters. First, we set up the tent camp with the cooking area and a latrine then we unpacked enough expedition equipment to make us comfortable while we developed the permanent camp. Leonard was anxious to get started on his building, and by the time Tag and I had off-loaded the pickup, Leonard was in the middle of building the headquarters floor.

Tag and I made several trips to town, dodging big salt trucks as we transported expedition equipment from the warehouse to the campsite. Every time we got back to the site with a load of equipment, we were amazed at the progress Leonard had made with the building. On one trip into town, I tried to tell Miguel about the drivers of the trucks that were running us off the road.

He laughed, and I'm not sure I completely understood what he told me, but if I got it right, he said some of the drivers only knew how to drive in a straight-line. Since the road was perfectly straight from the salt ponds to the dumping area, they wouldn't have to make any turns. He said that when they got to the dumping area and emptied the load, a man who could really drive the truck would turn it around and line it up with the "road. The "straight road driver" would get in and drive it back to the salt ponds. There, after the truck was loaded, another fully qualified driver would turn the truck around and line it up on the road. The "straight road driver" could now drive it back to the dumpsite. I thought Miguel might be pulling our legs, until on one trip, Tag and I saw the driver exchange at the dumpsite. After that we got well clear of the road, when we saw a truck coming!

ALL THE EXPEDITION EQUIPMENT MOVED TO THE LAGOON CAMPSITE.

LEONARD, BULDING OUR CAMPSITE HEADQUARTERS, WHERE WE WOULD MEET, EAT, AND DO LAB WORK.

EXPEDITION CAMPSITE COMPLETED. PHOTO TAKEN FROM THE HELICOPTER

CHAPTER 9
GHOST FLUTES OF OJO DE LIEBRE

The first day of building camp ended. We ate a canned supper and thought about getting ourselves situated for the night. Leonard was an older man in his late sixties, and Tag and I were about the same age. Leonard would be turning in early and Tag and I would want to stay up a while, talk, and maybe play some cards. We figured that Leonard would rest better and have some privacy if he had a tent to himself. Tag and I would be tent mates for the expedition.

Leonard was very tired from building all day and turned in right after supper. Tag and I sat out on the beach watching whales and enjoying the beautiful Baja sunset. When it finally got dark, Tag and I turned in for the night. It had been a long first day and we were both tired.

About 1:30 AM, Tag woke me up saying that there was something crawling around under the tent floor. "Did you hear that?" he said. "No," I answered, trying to listen while not yet fully awake. We were both listening, and in a few minutes, we could hear something making a scraping sound under the canvass tent floor. We turned on a couple of heavy-duty camp flashlights and looked around on the floor of the tent. There was nothing. As we were about to turn off the lights, the sound started again. We focused our lights on the area of the tent floor where the sound seemed to come from. Suddenly, there was movement. Something was crawling between the sand and the canvass floor. Tag spotted more movement and then another movement in a different area. Whatever they were, there were a lot of them! Once we were aware of them, we couldn't get back to sleep.

We lay there in the dark trying to ignore them, but they were too noisy and creepy and they begin to wear of our nerves. "Tag, are those things bothering you as much as they're bothering me?" I asked in a low voice. "Yes, I can't get to sleep with those things crawling around under the floor." "Me neither let's kill them!" I said. Both Tag and I got up and grabbed a boot. We shined our lights on the tent floor and whenever we saw movement we would pound on that spot with the boot.

It must have been a hilarious sight with Tag and me in our shorts crawling around on our hands and knees pounding the bejabbers out of whatever it was under the tent floor. We must have spent twenty minutes annihilating anything that moved. Finally, there was no more movement and the tent was quiet. Tag and I returned to our bunks and after a time we drifted off.

About 2:30 Tag woke me up again. "What is it? More critters?" I yawned. "No," Tag answered. "There's flute music coming from outside the tent!" "Flute music?" I said, still half asleep. "Yes, flute music. "Listen, it's coming from outside the tent." Beginning to wake up, I listened and in a few seconds, I distinctly heard about six notes of flute music. Everything was quiet for a minute and then I heard almost a complete musical scale up and down. It was coming from some sort of a flute-like instrument. Tag and I were now sitting up in our bunks totally perplexed and a little spooked. Who could be out there playing a flute now, at our remote campsite?

We knew Leonard didn't play any musical instrument, besides now he would be sound asleep. Tag suggested that maybe it was tourist campers that sometimes drive the Baja. Then he remembered something he read about the Baja and some bandit groups that still roamed the hills. I immediately got a flashback scene from the old Humphrey Bogart movie <u>Treasure of the Sierra Madre</u> and relayed my thoughts to Tag, saying that maybe there were several unshaven, rough looking bandits wearing crossed bullet bandoliers. One would be sitting on his horse playing the flute, waiting for us to come out of the tent. The leader would give us a big smile with one gold tooth gleaming in the moonlight. He would say that they were policemen and when we would ask them to show us their badges they would say "*Badges? We don't need no stinking badges*!" Tag laughed, but we were still a bit unnerved by the persistent flute music.

I took my pistol from its holster, checked the rounds in the 9-shot chamber. It was fully loaded. I motioned to Tag to get the powerful battery lantern. I slipped into my shorts and sandals and paused at the entrance of the tent to allow Tag to get into position. The flute music continued with its' haunting scales, and now it seemed to be a lot louder coming from just outside the tent.

Tag nodded that he was ready, and I threw back the tent door flap. The lantern beam illuminated the entire area in front of the tent and faded out into the dark desert landscape. There was nothing. Tag swung the lantern beam to both sides of the tent. Still nothing. Then we both stepped out of the tent into the night.

There was a cool brisk wind blowing, but the night temperature was still pleasant. A quick look about the camp revealed no flute-playing bandits. Now there was no sound, just a whisper of the night wind and the bright moon lighting up the desert and reflecting off the quiet waters of the lagoon. Tag and I were standing about six feet from the front of our tent staring out into the night scene when behind us from our tent came an entire scale of flute music. It startled both of us, and I whirled around ready to draw down on the flute-playing ghost!

Focusing the light on the corner of the tent and the place the music seemed to come from, Tag and I discovered the source of the phantom music. At each corner of our tent were aluminum tent poles that stabilized the corners of the tent. They were adjustable and had several adjustment holes drilled into one side making a flute of sorts out of the stabilizing poles. Two of the poles were aligned so that when the wind gusted a little, the air passing over the holes at right angles made sounds that resembled someone playing scales on a flute.

Tag walked over to one of our tent poles that was not aligned with the wind and rotated it 90 degrees. Instantly, a wind initiated melodic scale accompanied our other flute pole. I turned the remaining two poles with the wind direction and for a few moments we were serenaded with a symphony of random flute music. After a good laugh, we turned the tent poles to a position where the wind could not blow across the holes and we returned to our bunks. Having survived the tent critters and the ghost flutes of "Ojo de leibre" we finally got to sleep. Our sleep was restful and we dreamt of pleasant things, oblivious to what fate had in store for us over the next few weeks.

Alfonso Bedoya as "Gold Hat"

TREASURE OF THE SIERRA MADRE

'BADGES?? WE DON'T NEED NO STINKING BADGES!!"

CHAPTER 10
CAST OF CHARACTERS

The morning sun had barely crested the distant desert hills when the generator fired up. Leonard was already starting to work, and Tag and I were trying to get our eyes open. We sat up in our bunks cursing the noise and then we looked at each other and cracked up as we recalled the events of the night.

During the next few days, we set up a permanent camp and transferred all the expedition equipment from the warehouse in Guerrero Negro to laguna Ojo de liebre. The only thing we left in storage was the helicopter. When Gayle Neet, our pilot arrived, he would attach the blades and fly the helicopter from the warehouse out to the expedition site.

At the end of the first week, the camp was complete with a headquarters building, an outhouse, six 4-man tents, and various storage areas for equipment and supplies. Tag and I launched the Boston whaler and got to do some exploring up and down the labyrinth of channels of Scammon's Lagoon. Sadly, we found the remains of several Grey Whale calves that had washed up on some of the sandbars in the channels. They either died at birth or were not able to make it after birth. Some of them had several distinct bite marks from large sharks.

The shallow lagoon channels have an abundance of leopard sharks so Tag and I confined our swimming to the shallow water near the expedition camp. I did some free diving in one of the deeper channels, but a run-in with a couple of large sharks made the point that I was smaller than a newborn baby Grey whale. It reinforced my self-imposed restriction on any extensive free diving in these waters.

During the first week, we found that we would have to check our boots for scorpions and tarantula spiders and that there were poisonous snakes and Gila monsters that we wanted to avoid. We also discovered that the tent floor critters were small crabs that burrowed beneath the beach sand. With most of the Baja hazards identified, we started feeling at home.

Two more expedition members arrived during the second week. Dr. Thomas Poulter, a renowned biologist from Stanford University and Dr. Paul Dudley White, President Dwight Eisenhower's heart physician came in on the company DC-3. Tag and I met them at the airstrip and took them out to the expedition camp.

Dr. Poulter was an authority on recording and categorizing whale sounds. Dr. Poulter had garnered some notoriety in his younger days. It seemed he had hiked several miles into a camp in the Antarctic to rescue an ailing Admiral Byrd, the famous explorer. Dr. White was retired and had been invited to join the expedition by Dr. Spencer. Dr. White was an advocate of physical conditioning and brought along a bicycle, which he rode around camp and up and down the roads around the lagoon campsite. Dr. Poulter came to the expedition with a couple of suitcases that weighed a ton. Tag and I could barely carry them from the plane to the truck. Later we found that they contained heavy underwater cable for Dr. Poulters' sound listening stations. Dr. Poulter was a big man and although he was in his mid-sixties, he was exceptionally strong.

In the next few days, the rest of the expedition members arrived. There was Dr. Spencer and his friend Art Samuelson, Norman Simmons, a research technician, and Kelly Mc Collough, a whale and dolphin capture expert from Sea World in San Diego. All of them came by in the Salt company's' DC-3. Bill Garrett, our reconnaissance pilot, and Gayle Neet, our helicopter pilot, came in Bill's Piper Comanche. Bill landed the airplane on a temporary airstrip that we had made in the desert next to camp. The cast of characters was now complete.

After the expedition members were all settled, we had a couple of days of planning meetings. We laid out our strategy for conducting the study of the Grey whales. When the planning meetings were over, we prepared all the equipment that we would need during the expedition. We took Gayle to the warehouse so he could get the helicopter.

It took Gayle about five hours to set up and check the helicopter, and after some run-up tests he flew to the campsite and landed on our temporary helicopter pad made from wooden pallets. Because we now had a finished camp, an airplane, a helicopter and a landing strip. We dubbed the camp, the VMRC Research Station at Scammon's Lagoon and Garrison International Airport. Now, the research work could begin.

CHAPTER 11
FUN, PRANKS, AND SERIOUS BUSINESS

The first few weeks of the expedition were devoted to studying the movement of the whales and practicing our strategies for tranquilizing a Grey Whale, and our techniques for obtaining respiratory and blood samples. The exciting part of the activity was getting to fly in the helicopter. Since I was the chief diver on the expedition and had the best chance of surviving a helicopter crash in the lagoon, I was also named the expedition's choice to deliver a tranquilizer from the helicopter.

The plan was to locate a lone whale and fly close enough to deliver a tranquilizer dart and tagging buoy. To get close enough to the whale to place the dart efficiently, the helicopter had to follow the whale and hover just a few feet above the whale as it surfaced. Both Gayle and I were dressed for swimming, as the potential for a mishap was great. We had a well-rehearsed crash, ditch, escape plan.

If we lost power and the helicopter went in the water, the blades would still be turning, so we would have to wait until we sank to the bottom in the shallow lagoon and made sure that the blades had stopped turning before releasing our seat belts and leaving the helicopter. I was a seasoned diver with the ability to free dive to 100 feet and hold my breath for a long time, but Gayle didn't have that kind of aquatic ability.

I rigged two small SCUBA cylinders and mounted them where we could quickly access the second stage regulators in the event we went in the water. I also attached a diving facemask to each tank. I gave Gail some accelerated training in using SCUBA gear and donning a facemask and purging it from water. We took the Boston Whaler to a protected channel and practiced several simulated emergency ascent drills from a depth of 30 feet. Gayle was a fair swimmer and seemed to adapt to the underwater training well. I just hoped that we would never have to put our training to the test!

During the next few weeks, we conducted several studies and tested our respiratory and blood sampling equipment. We practiced a lot of low-level flying, while I shot at some floating targets with practice tranquilizer darts. We also worked out a method of safely deploying the tagging buoy and the line that would be attached to the large tranquilizer dart shot from the helicopter. We had rigged a make-shift launching platform on the helicopter. It held a large rubber buoy attached to 150 feet of carefully coiled Samson cord. The buoy and the cord were lightly taped to the platform so that when the tranquilizer dart was fired from the rifle launcher, the cord attached to the dart and the buoy would not get fouled on the helicopter. That would leave Gayle and me in a flying machine of highly unstable dynamic balance, attached to a twenty-five-ton whale! That was an "E" ticket ride neither Gayle nor I wanted to take.

After the days of preparation and experimenting, the evenings were quiet and restful and everyone would usually turn in around 9 PM. Sometimes Tag and I would sit up playing cards or just share our thoughts. One night after everyone was in bed and asleep, and the wind outside was still blowing gently, Tag and I just couldn't resist! We had previously adjusted all the tent poles so that the prevailing wind could not make flute music. But now was the perfect time to liberate the ghost flutes of Oho de leibre.

About 1:30 AM, we crept out our tent and quickly turned all the tent poles on three of the tents so that the holes were 90° to the wind. Almost immediately, the tent poles started their music. After we had all the tent poles aligned with the wind, we quickly slipped back into our tent and waited. The flute music was playing, softly at first, and with the number of tent poles we had tuned, it was a symphony of pole music! After a short time the wind picked up and the music got louder and louder. Tag and I were trying to keep from laughing. We were waiting with anticipation for some reaction from the other tent occupants.

After a couple minutes of loud flute music, we started to get our planned results. From one tent came the first reaction "Merrill are you awake?" "What is it?" came, Dr. Spencer's muffled response. "Merrill, do you hear that sound outside?" After a short pause, we heard "No, I don't" "What sound Art?" "It sounds like a bunch of flutes outside Merrill!" There was another short pause, then "Did you say there are flutes outside Art?" By now Tag and I are biting our blankets to stifle our laughter. Then Art responds, "Something's not right Merrill; there's a lot of flutes out there!" Where are they Art?" Dr. Spencer asked. "It sounds like they're right outside our tent Merrill!" "Yea, I can hear them. Who are they Art?" "I don't know but they're right outside our tent!" There was a loud shout! "Who's out there playing those flutes?" Then there came another voice from another tent "Yea who's out there playing that music?!"

Now Tag had rolled off his bunk on to the floor of the tent. He was lying on his back, peddling his feet in the air and rolling from side to side, tears were streaming down his face as he bit down hard on his blanket. The voices continued, "Alright, stop that music right now!" came a strong command from one of the tents. That was it. Tag went into convulsions. Now it was more than I could stand with the combination of comments coming from the tents, Tag rolling on the tent floor, and the flute poles going crazy with their wind symphony, I lost it and roared with laughter and didn't care who heard me. I literally laughed myself into exhaustion!

I finally got Tag to sober up, and we went over to the other tents. We confessed our practical joke and detuned all the flute poles. Everyone took the joke well after we explained that we were the first victims. After these many years, I talked to Tag the other day and reminded him of the flute poles. We both agreed that it was the best practical joke that either of us ever pulled off.

Another week of practice sessions in the helicopter gave us a chance to get familiar with the labyrinth of channels and shadow some of the whales for several miles. We hovered 20 to 50 feet above them as they meandered up and down the channels. While familiarizing ourselves with the channels and studying the whales diving and surfacing habits, we saw a lot of small leopard sharks and a couple of larger White tips or Mako sharks. The frequent sightings of these larger sharks dampened Gail's enthusiasm for our underwater helicopter escape practice sessions.

Large Grey Whale's run about 45 to 50 ft. in length and weigh approximately 25 tons. Their flukes are about 14 to 16 ft. wide, only a few feet shorter than our Boston Whaler boat. We learned the hard way that these huge animals are very agile, and can quickly reverse their direction underwater

One day, Kelly, the capture expert from Sea World, Tag, and I were appointed as a team to take our 17 foot Boston Whaler and get as close as we could to a Grey Whale. We three were selected as a team because we were the best swimmers and divers in the expedition. We were the youngest, most fearless, most foolish and therefore the most expendable! As we were getting ready to leave in the Whaler, Dr. Spencer asked if Art Samuelson could go with us to take photographs. It would be nice to have some photographic documentation of any exciting encounters, but Art didn't appear to be the rugged aquatic type. He might be somewhat of a liability if we were to be capsized by a whale. I think the team knew we might have to help Art.

About two hours later, we had located and were shadowing a large momma grey whale with a calf. We were trailing her within 25 to 40 yards. She would surface every 100 yards or so, keeping the baby whale very close to her head. Apparently, she didn't appreciate our company. On one dive, she disappeared for several minutes. We thought we had lost her when suddenly, Kelly shouted a warning! "She's turned around and headed right for us!"

The sight of that behemoth coming straight at our small boat was impressive, to say the least, we barely had time to react before the huge whale was upon us. She started her dive about 40 feet from our boat and I thought for sure that her flukes would hit the whaler and flip it over. I got ready for the impact and shouted, "Hang on everyone; we're going to get hit."

I had a quick vision of a long boat full of old whaling seamen being dashed to pieces by a huge whale and then eaten by sharks as portrayed in artwork of the book on the Scammon's Lagoon! I braced myself for the impending collision and thought about the sharks that might come to investigate the crash. The only consolation was that I could out swim anyone on the boat! The anticipated crash never came.

The whale was obviously not trying to hit the boat, but just dive under it to head for the open Lagoon. It was quite an experienced to have that huge mammal pass just a few feet under the boat. Just when I thought we'd escaped disaster, I heard Tag holler. "Watch out for the flukes!"

Too late, the flukes hit us and 20 to 30 gallons of water were thrown into the boat. The bulk of water hit Kelly and me, and I had to grab the side of the boat to keep from being knocked overboard! The impact of water and the turbulence of the whale's wake knocked everyone off their feet. After the big whale passed, we were all sitting in about an inch of water, soaking wet in a wild rocking boat!

"Wow, that was fun!" exclaimed Kelly, as he got to his feet "I thought we were whale fodder!" Tag said, wiping the salt water from his face. "It felt like shades of Moby Dick!" I added, as I struggled to stand up. Art was sitting in water, speechless, staring blankly after the departing whale. His impression of the experience was evidenced by his total loss of facial color. "I suggest we don't follow so close." advised Kelly. "That's a big ten four." I replied. Tag just nodded in agreement and we filed the experience away in our notes from whale shadowing 101!

DR. PAUL DUDDLY WHITE, DR. THOMAS POULTER AND ME AT THEIR ARRIVAL ON THE DC-3.

KELLY, TAG, AND ART GETTING THE BOSTON WHALER READY TO GO LOOK FOR SOME WHALES.

KELLY WITH TAG ON THE CAMERA AND A 47 FOOT 25 TON GREY WHALE CLOSE!

CHAPTER 12
THE WHALE / SNAKE FLIGHT

Three or four days later, Gayle and I were in the helicopter. We had located a huge gray whale with no young, and were following her closely at a very low altitude. The objective was to be in the proper position to deliver the tranquilizer dart effectively. The proper positions would mean that the helicopter would have to be about a third of the way back on the whales' body and about 15 feet above her as she rolled through the surface.

We had been tracking her for about 15 minutes, and she had breached several times. Apparently, she sensed the presence of the helicopter hovering above her and kept submerging before we could get into position for a proper shot.

As if it were a strategic move, the big whale sounded and disappeared for several minutes. Gayle kept the helicopter hovering just a few feet above the last boil of water which was made by the huge creature's flukes. We were both searching frantically for some sign of where the whale would surface. After a few moments, I had the distinct feeling I had been in this same situation a few days earlier in a boat!! Suddenly my peripheral vision caught movement in the water on our left rear quarter.

"She's up Gayle!" I shouted. "Behind us on the left". Gayle swung the helicopter to the left and I wasn't happy with what I saw!

The helicopter was now hovering about ten feet above the water and a whale 50 feet long weighing 25 tons with bad intentions was coming straight at us, full speed, about 30 yards away. When she was within fifty feet of us, she dove with her back arching sharply to get underwater right in front of the helicopter. As the whale's back rolled underwater directly in front of us, I could see that the huge flukes would breach about 15 feet from the helicopter.

I knew exactly what was going to happen and what I desperately needed to say to warn Gayle, but somehow my mind would not connect with my mouth to get out a coherent warning until it was too late. "Flukes," ----- flukes," "Water," I yelled! Then, finally I hollered, "Pull up," "Pull up," just as a wall of salt water rose from the channel and was coming at us. I don't think Gayle even heard my warnings, if he did; it wasn't nearly as motivating as the wall of water about to engulf us.

Gayle pulled up the little Hughes 269, but not nearly high enough or fast enough. Salt water washed into the cockpit and rocked the helicopter and spun it sideways. For a moment, we couldn't see anything out of the big bubble canopy except green water! As the water rolled off the canopy, I could see that we were still hovering about 6 feet above the channel. I silently thanked God! "Wow, she almost got us," exclaimed Gayle
"Sorry Gayle." I said. "I saw it coming and tried to warn you sooner, but I just couldn't get it out fast enough!"

Gayle lifted the helicopter up about 80 feet above the Lagoon, and we checked everything out. Except for being wet, we seemed to be ok. We were yakking about the incident and having a good laugh, when the engine coughed a couple of times and threatened to quit! Gayle looked very concerned, so I got even more concerned! We were still about one quarter mile out from the closest channel shore, and the water below us at that time was probably 20 to 30 feet deep. Gayle twisted a few knobs and flew the helicopter toward the nearest shore.

As the water got shallower, I could see several leopard sharks swimming along the channel floor. The engine coughed, sputtered again, and tried to die. Then, miraculously it roared back to life as Gayle flew it toward the beach. A third time, the engine almost died as we dropped to within 15 feet of the water, then another surge of power from the engine lifted us up about 30 feet and not a moment too soon; we were over the beach and onto the desert!

Just as I yelled, "We made it!" over the roar of the engine, it sputtered, coughed and died! -------- The silence of the engine was awesome! I heard Gayle utter a couple of expletives! At that moment, we were hovering about 40 ft. over the desert floor and a few seconds after the engine quit, we started down; way too fast, I thought. "Hang on!" Gayle shouted. "Right." I replied. We hit the ground with a thud, bounced the little and slid for about 6 feet to a stop in the sand and sagebrush. There were several boulders within three or four feet of us, but fortunately we didn't hit them.

We kicked up quite a bit of dust as we crashed, or *"auto-rotated"* to a landing, as Gayle like to call it. When the dust settled, we realized that we were OK and the helicopter didn't appear to be damaged either. "That was exciting!" I exclaimed. "Yeah," he replied. "a little too exciting!" Gayle was unbuckling his seatbelt and about to get out of the helicopter when I said, "Gayle, you better wait till I get out and you can get out on my side," I said in rather a strong suggestive voice. "Why not get out on my side?" Gayle asked. "Because, I just saw a huge rattlesnake go behind the boulder right next to the helicopter on your side! "Good call!" Gayle said as he waited for me to get out on my side.

There were several large rocks about 8 feet from my side of the helicopter and just beyond them I could see at least three more snakes, very large rattlesnakes. "Be very careful where you step." I warned Gayle. "It looks like we picked "Rattlesnake Riviera" for a crash-landing site. Oh, Sorry, our controlled "*auto-rotation*" site." Gayle grimaced and looked in the direction I was pointing so he could see the other snakes. We worked our way carefully out in front of the helicopter and onto a large open area devoid of sagebrush or rocks that could hide the snakes.

A few minutes later, the Boston whaler, with Tag and Kelly landed at the beach about 40 yards from us. When they turned off the boat motor; we yelled at them to watch out for the rattlesnakes! Neither Tag nor Kelly made any attempt to get out of the boat after our announcement. Gayle and I carefully worked our way to the boat, and we all returned to camp to get some snake repellent equipment and some tools to fix the helicopter. Everyone at camp was impressed with our story of how a whale can destroy a helicopter! Gayle and I kind of took the experience in stride, but we both knew we were damn lucky! All The expedition flights after that were very exciting, but nothing like the whale/snake flight.

HUGHES 269 HELICOPTER WITH ME AND THE PILOT GAIL NEET. BOTH OF US WERE DRESSED FOR SWIMMING!

ABOUT 15 FEET ABOVE THE WATER IN THE HELICOPTER FOLOWING A BIG GREY WHALE

6 FOOT LEOPARD SHARK. THERE WERE LOTS OF SHARKS AROUND

CHAPTER 13
PISTOLARO DE BAJA

One last story from the Grey Whale expedition revolves around the pistol I had taken with me to Mexico. When we weren't conducting research, or doing camp chores, Tag and I would take our pistols and find targets to shoot. Sometimes we would hunt ducks, although I don't remember that we ever got one. Mostly, we would just practice fast draw and shoot at targets.

Another of our pastimes was roaming the beaches of the lagoon. We discovered that the hard sun baked mud beaches contained a large amount of fossilized shark teeth. Some of the ones we found measured eight inches across the top and were about ten inches long. Now this is a single Tooth! I believe the area was once a sea in the Devonian Period. Some of the teeth probably belonged to prehistoric sharks like the C Megalodon that inhabited the waters during that time. It was a shark that paleontologists estimated to be as much as 60 to 100feet long and weigh 100 tons. A monster shark of that size with a mouth full of teeth as large as the big one that I just described, would have made salt water sports very unpopular!

One day when we had a lull in the research work, Tag and I decided to go up the beach to hunt for shark teeth. Victor, our Mexican camp laborer was also off duty and wanted to go along with us. I welcomed his company because it gave me a change to practice my Spanish, and for Victor to learn more English.

Victor was a tall, stoic, man about 38 years old, I guessed. His face was brown and withered from the severe environment of ocean, sun and desert. He wore a pair of old patched up tan pants and a light blue cotton work shirt. On his bare feet, he wore an old pair of leather sandals and on his head, a dirty old straw hat. He looked like a typical south of the border character in an old western movie.

Earlier that afternoon, Tag and I had been practicing our quick draw shooting so both of us were wearing our pistols as we started off up the beach. I was wearing my gun belt with the ornate western buckle and had the pistol holster slung low on my hip and tied down to my leg for fast draw shooting. I had on a worn pair of jeans and a long sleeve shirt with a rip in it. I had a large red bandanna tied around my neck and I had about a three-day growth of beard, so I probably looked like an old western movie character myself.

Tag, Victor and I wandered about a mile and a half up the beach and spent a few hours looking for sharks' teeth. We found several small and medium sized teeth and after tiring of the search, we started back to camp. Instead of walking along the beach on the hard iron-shore mud, we moved up on to the desert plateau that ran within twenty or thirty yards of the beach.

We were walking along talking, and had gone about a hundred yards when we came upon a large outcropping of desert rock. About thirty yards from the rocks, Victor suddenly halted and grabbed my left arm. "Tarantula!" he exclaimed and pointed straight ahead to a couple of large boulders. There, crawling across one of the big rocks was a huge Tarantula spider nearly the size of my fist. "Tarantula!" Victor repeated as he again motioned toward the big spider.

Perhaps at that moment, some primitive instinct for survival or challenge of combat took over my normally reserved thinking processes. Without a moment's hesitation, I drew on the tarantula. Since I had been practicing quick draw for several days, the gun came up lightning quick, at least lightning quick for me. Just as the pistol leveled, I squeezed off a shot. In the blink of an eye, thirty yards away, the huge spider was blown off the rock!

No one could have been more surprised than I was when I hit the spider from that distance. Then I remembered that three of the nine bullets were 22-caliber birdshot. Those bullets contained many small lead pellets and would expand to a large pattern at 30 yards. Obviously, one of the many pellets had hit the spider blowing it off the rock. Immediately after the shot, I did a fancy spin with the pistol and dropped it back into its holster.

The entire sequence of the shot from holster to holster couldn't have taken more than a couple of seconds! What Victor witnessed was a lightning fast shot from the hip that took out the moving spider at 30 yards. What he didn't know was that the spider had been hit by huge pattern of birdshot!

After I had holstered the pistol, I looked at Tag. He gave me big thumbs up and I smiled and just walked on as if it was nothing. It never occurred to me that Victor was highly impressed by the spectacle. I never spoke to Victor about shooting the spider, and he never discussed it with me.

A couple of days after the spider shooting incident, Tag and I drove the pickup into town to get groceries and supplies from the store. We had both been practicing fast draw shooting just before we left camp to go to town and both of us were still wearing our pistols when we got there. We were reluctant to leave our guns in the truck for fear that they might be stolen. We had seen other men carrying rifles in to the cantina in town before. We assumed there was no law or ordinance against carrying a weapon so we wore them into the store when we went to get our groceries.

The lady in the store was not the normal, happy, and friendly person we were used to dealing with. That day, she was reserved, formal, and extremely apologetic for any discrepancies in our order. She acted very nervous. It was about 4:30 in the afternoon. It was very hot, Tag and I were thirsty and ready for a cold beer. I told the lady to box up our supplies and we would pick them up after we came back from having a drink at the Cantina. She nodded and obediently started packing up the food and supplies. After we paid her, we left the store and headed for the Cantina down the street.

As Tag and I walked out of the store and started down the street, I looked back and caught the store lady staring after us from the window. I thought it was odd, the way she watched us as we walked away toward the Cantina. I mentioned to Tag that I thought she acted strange. He agreed and suggested that perhaps she was just having a bad day.

The sidewalk to the Cantina was more boardwalk and dirt than concrete. About a block ahead, we saw two men and woman laughing and talking. They were coming toward us on our side of the street, but when they saw us, they stopped talking and quickly crossed to the other side of the street. I asked Tag if he was beginning to feel like a foreigner. When the people had passed, they stopped and stared after us as we walked the rest of the way to the Cantina.

"That was Strange!" I remarked to Tag. "We must be a novelty." He nodded in agreement. The Cantina could have easily taken its rightful place in any old western movie. It was complete with a rickety board sidewalk leading up to a set of louvered wooden swinging bar doors. When we entered the Cantina, there were about seven men seated at the tables talking and drinking beer, and as we pushed through the Cantina doors, all their conversations fell silent. Every eye was focused on us. Tag and I felt very conspicuous as we walked up to the bar. The bar floor was warped and it creaked as we walked across it, making us feel even more conspicuous.

The Cantina was quite small. There were about nine old wooden tables with several chairs placed about the room. At one end of the room was an old beat up, heavy built, wooden bar straight out of the 18th-century. The back-bar shelf contained several bottles of various kinds of whiskey and a couple of bottles of wine. Our reflections coming from the huge bar mirror were distorted, probably from warping of the glass due to aging and heat. There was a row of beer mugs lined up on the back bar.

The bartender was an older man with a white beard. He was wearing a bartender's apron and a black vest. His name was Samuel and I had met him when I stopped in for a beer one other time. "Olla Samuel" "two cold beers please" I said in my poor Spanish. "Si Senior'" he replied, nervously and hurried to a cooler to get two cold beers. Our bartender, who was normally friendly and talkative, was now strangely quiet. After he got us our beers he excused himself to do some chores, and went a room in the back of the bar.

As we sat at the bar drinking our beer, I heard the doors behind us swing open and closed several times and I could see in the mirror, several men leaving the Cantina. We had only taken a few sips of our beer, when we slowly turned around to see that the entire Cantina was now empty. After finishing our beers, we waited a long time for the bartender too return. But he didn't even come back to collect his money. Both Tag and I were starting to feel like ugly Americans. I figured that maybe we had offended someone at some other time when we had been in town, and the word was out. Feeling very uncomfortable, I put the beer money and a very large tip on the bar, and Tag and I left the Cantina.

We picked up the food and supplies from the grocery store and drove the 15 miles back to the expedition campsite. During the drive, Tag and I remarked about the strange treatment we had experienced in town and we figured we could ask Victor about it when he returned to the camp after his day off.

The next day after our trip into town, Mr. Bremner, a manager from the salt company visited us at the campsite. He had just returned from a vacation in the United States and, he spoke perfect English. Dr. Spencer was making the rounds introducing Mr. Bremner to all the members of the expedition. When he got to me, Mr. Bremner exclaimed,

"Oh. This is Spence! Spence is becoming very famous in Baja you know!" Both Dr. Spencer and I were very surprised by his comment, and totally confused about what he meant?

Dr. Spencer asked him to explain. Mr. Bremner told us that Victor was telling anyone in town who would listen to him that he saw Spence draw a pistol like lightning, shoot from the hip, and blow a tarantula spider off a rock at 40 yards He is telling everyone that Spence is a tough hombre, the macho Pistolaro of all Baja!

My face must've turned beet red from embarrassment, and I shook my head in disbelief! "Now, I know why the people in town acted so strange when Tag and I went in for supplies yesterday!" I said. "Yes." Mr. Bremner answered, "Because, you were both wearing the pistols into town, they were afraid of you and just wanted to stay out of your way! No one wanted to take a chance of offending you at the Cantina!" Now, the strange actions of the townspeople toward Tag and me made sense. And I was even more embarrassed!

I told Mr. Bremner and Dr. Spencer the story of the tarantula shot and they both had a good laugh! When Mr. Brunner stopped laughing, he gave me a serious look and said, "You know Spence. There are still a few renegade outlaw bands roaming the hills of the

Baja. I hope one of their Pistolaros doesn't hear about you and come to make a name for himself.

I wasn't sure if Mr. Bremner was pulling my leg or if there were some of those guys out there in the hills, but just in case I said. "Mr. Bremner, I'll explain to Victor how I really shot that spider and I would really appreciate it if you could pass the word in town that the pistolaro of Ojo de leibre has hung up his guns and left the country! Mr. Bremner and Dr. Spencer broke up laughing again.

After Mr. Bremner left, Dr. Spencer couldn't wait to tell rest of the expedition members about the Tag and I terrorizing the town with our 22 pistols. Both of us felt bad about the incident. Neither Tag nor I practiced our fast draws after that day, and we never wore the gun belts around camp or anywhere else. The pistolaros of Ojo de liebre had retired!

During the remainder of the expedition, our research work went smoothly, and we could accomplish most of our scientific goals. Dr. Spencer got his whale physiology data. Dr. Poulter captured lots of whale sounds with his equipment and would analyze the meaning of those sounds when he got back to his research laboratory at Menlo Park. For the rest of us that served on the expedition; it was an exciting adventure.

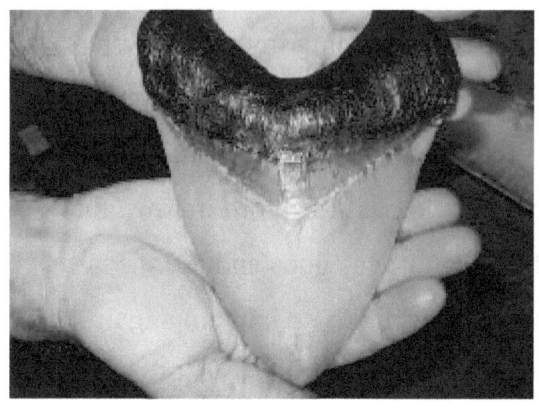

WHY OCEAN WATER SPORTS WERE NOT POPULAR MILLIONS OF YEARS AGO!!

DESERT TRANTULA

A REAL PISTOLARO DE BAJA. ONE I WANTED TO AVOID!!

CHAPTER 14
THE PERCEPTION

Our National Geographic Gray Whale expedition was a great adventure. The month and a half we spent at 'Oho de Leibre" was fun, educational, and exciting, but I was anxious to get back to Seattle and my research work on treating decompression sickness. After the next few months, we were awarded an NIH grant and a grant from the research center to continue my work and to develop a Diving Physiology research laboratory. The research was progressing, and I was busy conducting animal tests as well as writing and rewriting research papers. Dr. Spencer was developing protocol for his work on measuring blood flow with the Doppler equipment.

One day I happen to pass through one of the laboratories, where Dr. Spencer and his equipment technician Norm Simmons were calibrating some Doppler transducer cuffs. I know that Transducer cuffs sounds complicated, but it's not! They are just various sized round Styrofoam collars that contain two small crystals. The crystals act as a sound transmitter and a receiver. The collar halves are hinged together. They can be opened like a clam shell, and placed around a blood vessel. When the cuff is placed around an artery or a vein, the transmitter crystal beams a sound signal at moving blood cells flowing though the blood vessel. The sound beam is angled so that it bounces off the blood cells and returns to the receiver crystal. Because the blood cells are moving, the sound beam strikes the moving cell at one place and returns to the receiver from a slightly different place, due to the movement of the cell. This produces a change in the characteristic of the sound wave. The change in sound from a moving source is called the "Doppler Shift".

Everyone experiences the "Doppler shift" when they hear the whistle of a moving train fading from a high-pitched sound to a low sound as the train moves away into the distance. With the aid of electronic equipment, shifts in the sound can determine the speed of the train or in our case the speed of the blood flowing through a vessel. Knowing what the normal speed should be one could calculate the amount of blood flowing through the vessel, and then determine any restrictions or blockage. One could also locate where the blockage might be found.

Dr. Spencer's early calibration process utilized a tall glass cylinder about one inch in diameter and about ten inches tall. It was filled with a salt-water solution. The Styrofoam collar, containing the transmitter and receiver was placed around the glass cylinder, and then slid up and down. This produced a shifted signal that bounced off the particles in the salt water; much like blood flowing through a vein or artery. I stopped a moment to watch them as they conducted the tests. A wooshing sound was heard over the speakers form the salt particles as the cuff was moved up and down the glass cylinder. Intermittently, the whooshing sound was interrupted by a chirping sound or a series of brief chirps.

I asked Dr. Spencer, what made the chirping sounds and he said they were caused by small microscopic air bubbles, passing through the sound beam. "Oh, I said, nodding, "you mean, it changes sound when the tiny bubbles pass through the sound beam?" "That's right," Dr. Spencer confirmed as he continued his calibration. I stood watching them do their tests for a few minutes; then I started to leave the laboratory. As I walked toward the door, the resonating sound of the chirping bubbles switched on the proverbial *"idea light bulb"* in my brain.

Dr. Albert Bhenke, a famous naval diving medical officer, known as the forefather of submarine medicine, theorized that decompression sickness *"the bends"* was caused by compressed gas expanding and developing small microscopic bubbles in the blood and tissue of the diver. As the diver ascends from a deep dive, the bubbles grow, block crucial blood flow, and cause nerve and tissue damage. All preventions and treatments used at that time for decompression sickness, indicated that Dr. Bhenkes' theory was right, but because small bubbles could not be seen or detected in the human body under diving conditions, it was still a theory.

What if the Doppler cuff could be used to detect small gas bubbles in the blood of a diver undergoing decompression from a long, deep dive? My mind raced over many possibilities, and my excitement grew moment by moment. I stopped at the Lab door and walked back to Dr. Spencer. "What if we used the bubble detection capability of the Doppler cuff to prove Dr. Bhenkes' theory about the so-called "silent bubbles" that cause decompression sickness?" I asked.

Dr. Spencer was heavily focused on his calibration process, but the question I posed broke through his concentration like a lightning bolt. In a second his eyes met mine, and his face radiated a look of excited acknowledgement. He was the consummate researcher and possessed great Powers of correlation. He immediately grasped the significance of my question. "Spence, what a great idea. Go jot down some thoughts on what tests we could conduct to prove the theory."

His excitement was contagious and I went back to my office pretty jazzed up myself! The prospect of proving the bubble theory was an exciting challenge and if the Doppler would identify small bubbles in the blood, as well as it identified small bubbles in the calibration water, we would be the first researchers to hear and confirm Dr. Bhenkes' so-called "silent bubbles".

To detect and measure blood bubbles in a diver with the Doppler system, the Styrofoam transducer cuffs would have to be surgically Implanted on some very major blood vessels. One cuff would need to be around the large artery that leads directly from the heart to the lower extremities of the body, it is called the <u>Descending thoracic aorta</u>. Another cuff would have to be implanted around the large vessel that returns blood back to the heart from the lower extremities; this is the <u>Inferior vena cava</u>. A smaller cuff would have to be implanted on a large vessel located near the groin that returns blood to the heart from the leg and feet. This vessel is called the

<u>Femoral vein</u>. Due to the experimental nature of the surgery and the risk of severe decompression sickness, it was not possible to use a human diver. We decided that we could use a sheep for the test. A sheep is a good analog for a human because both the blood vascular system and the thoracic anatomy is quite similar.

During the next few weeks, Dr. Spencer and I had several meetings. We planned the surgery and the decompression dive profile that we would use to do the bubble experiment. Up to this time it had not occurred to me who would do the sheep surgery. I assumed it would be a Veterinary surgeon.

One day I asked Dr. Spencer who would do the surgery required for the experiment. "You will", came his matter-of-fact reply. My mind went temporarily numb with surprise! "But that's major thoracic surgery and I don't know how to do a surgery like that" I exclaimed. Dr. Spencer looked at me with a Confident smile "You'll learn", he said. At that I was just too dumbfounded to answer so I mentally resigned myself to follow Dr. Spencer's lead. Dr. Spencer assigned Ramon Gonzalez, a research physiologist at our Research Center to plan and oversee the animal surgery, and he asked Leonard Lockett, to secure a large healthy sheep for the surgery.

Dr. Spencer and I decided to use a decompression profile that was on the border between the shallower depths on the standard decompression table and the deeper depths of the exceptional exposure tables. We decided that after the sheep had recovered from surgery and was healthy and strong, and the implanted blood flow transducers were working properly, we would perform a simulated dive in the decompression chamber.

We would compress a sheep to a depth equivalent to 200 feet of seawater for 60 minutes, and then bring the animal up at the recommended rate of ascent of 60 feet per minute to a depth of 60 feet. This was the first stop depth that the Navy specifies in their decompression table. We would stop at this depth for the required time. We would then decrease the pressure to simulate subsequent stops at decreasing depths for various times specified in the Navy table. These stops would allow the compressed gas in the diver, or in this case the sheep to gradually escape without developing bubbles, which form in the blood and cause decompression sickness.

Even though we were using the U.S Navy operational decompression tables for navy divers, those tables were not a hundred percent foolproof. A small percent could still wind up with decompression sickness on a dive to 200 feet for 60 minute. Our research was designed to show whether any bubbles were formed in the blood from such a dive profile, and whether they were formed first in the lower extremities. We also wanted to see how much bubble formation there might be, and whether the sheep would show any objective signs of decompression sickness.

Once our experimental protocol was finalized and recorded, Dr. Spencer signed various tasks to the research team. I was still apprehensive about the prospects of Ramon and I performing the sheep surgery. I had some surgical training background working with Dr. Johnston, but this was major thoracic surgery. I had no knowledge or experience for this type of major surgery, and didn't know where to start! Dr. Spencer said Ramon and I could observe some thoracic surgeries at the hospital. Dr. Frank Henry, a prominent Seattle Thoracic Surgeon associated with the research center offered to take us under his wing and help us plan, study and practice for the procedures we had to perform.

The research center had a complete surgical suite, with an operating table, surgical lights, anesthesia administration equipment, a full set of surgical instruments, respiration and heart monitors, emergency equipment, and everything we might need to perform the surgical procedure. With such a facility, we could provide the same consideration given to a human operation. We were also able to draw on any equipment from the hospital or expert advice and guidance from Mason clinic surgeons.

When the implants were in and the sheep was healthy, Dr. Spencer and I would use a large decompression chamber made available to us by a company currently providing decompression chamber operations for a metropolitan sewer tunneling project. Using their chamber would allow us to perform the simulated 200-foot dive necessary to complete the experiment.

CHAPTER 15
DIVINE PROVIDENCE

During the next few weeks we refined our experimental plans while Ramon and I studied and trained to perform the surgery. Ramon was very knowledgeable on the anatomy and physiology of the animal. We both spent some time observing some thoracic surgeries and surgical techniques at the hospital. While we were training, I was thinking that I would be Ramon's assistant on the surgery, and I began to feel comfortable and competent to assist.

After a few weeks of preparation, we were ready and scheduled the surgery for about a week out. During that week, Ramon and Dr. Spencer did some exams and blood work on the sheep. I prepared all the instruments for sterilization. The instruments were washed in a prep solution, dried and wrapped in a clean cloth packaging to be autoclaved, a method of sterilizing by heat.

On the morning of the surgery, Ramon and I arrived early and scrubbed in. Leonard brought in the sheep, whom we named "Bubbles." All the physicians who were on our advisory team were notified that we were starting the operation. Our surgical team was comprised of the following members Ramon, Leonard, John Patton, and Roland White John and Roland were divers I had trained and student interns of the Diving Physiology Research Laboratory.

Ramon administered the anesthesia and operated the respiratory and vital sign monitoring equipment. When the sheep was fully anesthetized, and we had sterilized and prepared the surgical area, I asked Ramon what he wanted me to do.

"I can have better control over the monitoring and the procedure if you do the surgery" he said. His matter-of-fact demeanor had an immediate numbing effect on my thoughts.

"You mean you want me to operate!?" I asked, rather surprised.

"Yes," he answered. "I've been watching you in training, and I know you can do it." Just follow my direction, and let's get started." I wasn't quite as convinced as Ramon was about my surgical ability and steady hand, but his solid confidence bolstered mine. I nodded a somewhat reluctant "OK," picked up the scalpel and Ramón outlined the first incision point.

It was about 9:00 AM when we started the procedure. It seemed like everything we did took forever. I got a little nervous during the critical part of the surgery which was getting the main blood vessels exposed so we could implant the Doppler cuffs. Ramon was as steady as a rock, giving me continuous instruction and guiding my actions. The surgery was long and painstaking. Experienced surgeons could have completed the operation in half the time it took us to do it, but we were being very careful and had to take it slow.

About two hours into the procedure, we had exposed the two major blood vessels in the chest that we wanted to fit with Doppler cuffs. They were the Inferior vena cava and the descending thoracic aorta. The vena cava is a large blood vessel that brings circulated blood from the lower extremities to one half of the heart to be pumped through the lungs and returned to the other side of the heart to be pumped down the descending thoracic aorta to a large blood vessel that supplies the lower extremities. The cuffs on these two blood vessels would let us listen for bubbles that were developing in the bloodstream.

If there were micro bubbles from decompression, we wanted to know when they first occurred and where they occurred. When the two cuffs were implanted, our technician Norm Simmons came in with the Doppler monitoring equipment and tested the blood flow cuffs. They were working perfectly. Ramon and I went to work immediately closing the surgical site; after what seemed like forever. we had completed the first of the two required surgical procedures. At this point I had acquired a great deal of respect for surgeons who spend hours working over a patient on the operating table who was on the verge life or death.

Ramon and I took a brief break before starting the next procedure. Ramon made some adjustments to the anesthesia and closely checked respiration and vital signs to make sure that "Bubbles was OK. After the few minutes of rest Ramon and I started the next procedure I felt more relaxed and confident about this procedure because it was to be a relatively simple surgery to the sheep's groin to expose the femoral vein, the large vein that transports most of the circulated blood from the leg back to the heart. By placing a Doppler cuff around this vein, we hoped to determine if micro bubbles were first formed in the lower extremities. Exposure of this blood vessel was less of a procedure than the one we had just completed.

Within the hour we had the blood vessel exposed and again Ramon guided my every move. We had just installed and tested the Doppler cuff and were about to finish up and close, when I noticed a small blood vessel bleeding heavily near the implant site. When surgeons have a "*bleeder*" as they call it, they cauterize the blood vessel that is bleeding by applying an electric device called a "bovie" to the metal clamp holding the bleeder closed, this sears the tissue and stops the bleeding; sort of like the old western movies, when after the arrow was removed, the wound was sealed with a red-hot knife blade while the cowboy was told to "*bite the bullet*".

Either because of a hasty attempt to apply the "bovie," or my growing fatigue, I accidentally let the "bovie" slip off the clamp, it burned a large hole in the femoral vein an inch or so above our newly implanted cuff! For an eternally long second, I was in shock! Then, the shock turned to panic! Even before my mind could recover enough to think of calling for a vein clamp, Ramón, who had already pinched off the bleeder with his sterile gloved fingers, thrust one into my hand. "Clamp it!" he said. I quickly responded and clamped the vein on the supply side.

"I got it," I said. I then took another clamp from the instrument table and clamped the other side of the torn vein.

With the bleeding stopped and the situation temporarily under control, Ramon and I looked at each other and both realized that we had a critical situation. I had accidentally damaged a crucial blood vessel. If we couldn't repair the damage, the whole surgery would be lost and the sheep would be in serious trouble.

Our problem was that performing a vein repair required the hand of a specialist in rerouting and repairing blood vessels. What we desperately needed right now was a vascular surgeon. Now, neither Ramon nor I could remotely qualify to do any kind of a repair that would insure the sheep's successful recovery. We realized we were in deep sheep do-do! We began to discuss some possible options. Now, if anyone ever asks me if I believe in divine providence the answer will be a resounding "yes!"

As Ramon and I were standing there gloved and gowned contemplating our fate and the fate of Bubbles, the main door to the surgical lab opened. I looked around to see the head and shoulders of my Lewiston Idaho High School classmate and friend Bob Morrell. Dr. Bob Morrell. Dr. Bob Morrell the vascular surgeon, who was doing his residency at the mason clinic. He had been looking for another doctor who he thought might be in our lab. "Bob, am I glad to see you!" I exclaimed. We have a major problem! We are nearly five hours into the surgical experiment with this sheep and I just blew into the femoral vein with the "bovie!" Can you help us?"

Bob entered the lab, walked over to the surgical table and surveyed the damage to the vein. Then he walked over to the phone, called his office at the clinic across the street and asked someone to bring over his optical equipment and some small sutures (stitching thread) that he uses in vascular surgery.

When his equipment arrived, Bob scrubbed-in and performed a professional repair of Bubbles damaged femoral vein. When the clamps were released, there was no leakage and the Doppler was tested to show normal blood flow. Ramon and I thanked Bob for saving our butts and our mutton. Bob smiled and said "Anything for a brother Bengal! The Bengal Tiger was our Lewiston, Idaho high school mascot. Bob left us to the job of closing the surgical site and after about 30 minutes the procedure was complete. Now, Ramon had to get Bubbles off anesthesia and into a recovery mode. Leonard Lockett came into the lab to assist Ramon while John Patton assisted me in cleaning up the surgical area.

When Bubbles was stable in recovery, we turned her over to Leonard who would keep an eye on her throughout the remainder of the evening. We had made previous arrangements with a Veterinarian that sometimes worked with the research center. He would consult on any post-operative complications. As Ramon and I took off our surgical dress, we looked at each other and simultaneously, a large smile of relief appeared on both our faces. We shook hands and both agreed that it had been quite a day.

After Ramon left the surgical suite, I stood alone in the room and mentally replayed some scenes from the experience of the day! I crossed my fingers and said a silent prayer for Dr. Morrell's' special intervention and "Bubbles" successful recovery. Suddenly I was very tired and felt in serious need of a scotch and water!

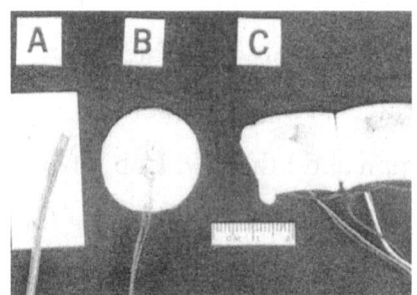

DOPPLER TRANSDUCERS. WE IMPLANTED THREE OF THE ONE ON THE RIGHT IN BUBBLES

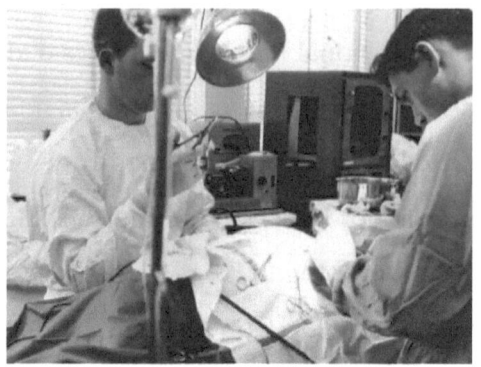

JOHN PATTON AND ME PREPARING BUBBLES FOR THE IMPLANTS.

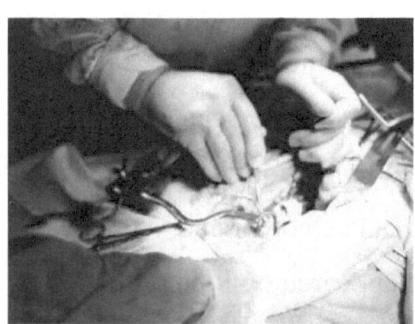

IMPLANTING THE DOPPLER CUFF AROUND THE MAJOR BLOOD VESSELS

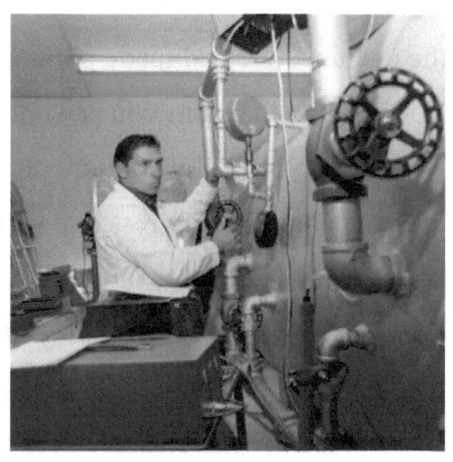

THE DECOMPRESSION CHAMBER WE USED FOR THE DOPPLER SHEEP EXPERIMENT

CHAPTER 16
TIME TO TEST

Bubbles' recovery went faster and much better than we thought it would and in about 50 days she was deemed healthy enough to participate in the decompression bubble experiment. The experimental dive took place in the decompression chamber. Dr. Spencer, Norm Simmons and I conducted the procedure that proved to be a milestone in the field of Submarine Medicine!

After compressing Bubbles to an equivalent seawater depth of 200 feet for sixty minutes, the pressure was reduced to simulate the ascent rate of a diver at sixty feet per minute. This was the recommended "not to exceed" rate specified on the Navy decompression tables. The first decompression stop on the Navy tables was at a depth of sixty feet. Before the ascent began, the Doppler recorder was turned on and you could hear the normal "whooshing" sound of the blood passing through the implanted Doppler cuffs.

We listened intently as we monitored the blood flow during the initial ascent to the first decompression stop. The depth was just passing 100 feet when we heard the first chirp, the characteristic sound of a gas bubble passing through the cuff. At a depth of 97 feet, more chirps and then a continuous building of bubble chirps to a crescendo. At the Navy table 60 foot stop the sheep's blood was filled with small bubbles. At this point, the experiment was terminated and decompression treatment procedures were started to relieve any pain and prevent permanent damage to "Bubbles". The recompression treatment was successful and after several days of rest and recovery, "Bubbles appeared normal and was released to live out the rest of her life with a regional herd of sheep. No one would probably ever know that this small sheep had made a major contribution to the field of submarine medicine.

The immediate result of the experiment was our realization that all the decompression tables including our U.S Navy tables, might have been missing a crucial factor! The tables were calculated using a model of nitrogen gas diffusion and had no consideration for bubbles existing in the blood prior to the stops required to prevent bubble formation. This landmark experiment, gave rise to a host of subsequent studies and modifications of diving decompression procedures.

My goal of helping to make a significant contribution to the field of submarine medicine had been fulfilled. Notoriety and fallout from the bubble experiment led to other significant studies, and I had the privilege and pleasure of traveling with Dr. Spencer to several national and international conferences on diving physiology and medicine. We gave presentations on our research, and served on discussion panels with well-known experts in the field of submarine medicine.

I continued my studies and research at VMRC for three years, during which time I was engrossed in the subject of diving physiology and participated with the national and international community of scientists in that field. At times, I would read five to 10 research papers, a week to keep up with the latest findings. I was asked to be a guest lecturer on the physiology and medical problems of commercial and sport divers to the occupational medicine students and staff at the University of Washington medical school.

During the next year, we had several notable visitors at Virginia Mason research center. One of those visitors was Dr. Herbert Saltzman from the Duke University School of Medicine. After spending two weeks with us and observing our research, Dr. Saltzman and I got to be good friends. Dr. Saltzman was a Dean at the Duke University medical school. About two weeks after his visit to the research center, I received a letter from him asking if I would like to continue my studies and work at Duke in their M.D./ PhD program. I was overwhelmed by the offer, but the problem of the position that I was offered was that I didn't even have a baccalaureate degree.

I called Dr. Saltzman and thanked him for his kind offer and informed him of my lack of academic credentials. There was a brief pause on the phone, and then he said, "Maybe we could work something out for you. Would you be interested then?" I told them that I would certainly consider the situation! During the following week, I thought seriously about the offer. I knew that there would be a lot of intense work on my part in a lot of sacrifice for my family.

Susan was showing disturbing symptoms and kidney problems with her severe diabetic condition. My two sons were now 4 and 6 years old, and I was deeply committed to the research projects at the research center. After some soul searching, I decided that I didn't necessarily want to be a doctor! I just wanted to know the things that they knew; learn more about the physiology and medicine of diving, and function at the level of a medical doctor or a PhD. I figured that I was already doing that!

Several days later, I called Dr. Saltzman and thanked him for his confidence and his kind offer. I told him that my current situation would preclude making that kind of a commitment. He said he understood and that if I should change my mind to call him.

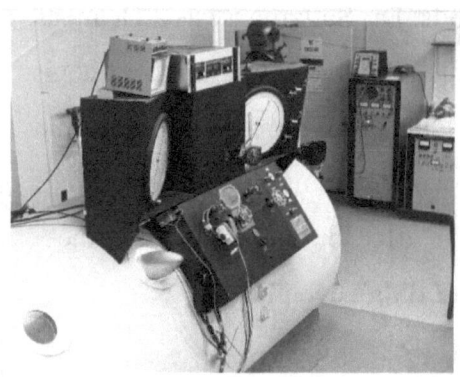

OUR FIRST NEW DECOMPRESSION CHAMBER IN THE DIVING PHYSIOLOGY RESEARCH LABORATORY.

DEVELOPMENT OF BUBBLES IN VENOUS AND ARTERIAL BLOOD DURING HYPERBARIC DECOMPRESSION*

Merrill P. Spencer, M.D.

and

Spencer D. Campbell

Virginia Mason Research Center

FIRST PUBLICATION OF THE DOPPLER RSEARCH DONE WITH THE SHEEP DECOMPRESSION EXPERIMENT. PUBLISHED IN THE BULLETIN OF THE MASON CLINIC

CHAPTER 17
RETURN TO RESEARCH

During the next year, our research work became quite well-known and we added some new members to our Board of advisers for the Diving Physiology Research program. One of the new advisors was Mr. John Lindbergh, son of the famous aviator Charles Lindbergh. John was well-known in his own right in the field of diving. He had been a Naval Diving Officer and had participated in some of the first civilian deep underwater habitat programs.

John was a mild-mannered, soft-spoken man with a focus and wisdom that was extremely rare. He had a special insight and a gift for applying a simple and direct approach to a problem that other researchers and traditional academicians would unnecessarily complicate! He and I were a lot alike in that respect, and we immediately hit it off and became good friends.

John and I made several experimental dives together in the chamber and in open water. He helped us design our new decompression chamber and gave us ideas on several approaches for our research. He also provided a valuable liaison between Virginia Mason research center and the researchers at Union Carbide Inc. and the U.S. Navy.

One gratifying experience that I had as Director of the diving physiology laboratory, was a weeklong visit from Dr. Albert

Bhenke, the forefather of submarine medicine. Our research had proven Dr. Bhenke's theories about silent Bubbles that cause the bands. He wanted to meet us and see what else we were doing. It was a great treat to get to spend time with someone I had admired in the field of submarine medicine. Dr. Bhenke was a gracious man with a lot of knowledge, and we were privilege to hear some great stories from the early Navy diving days. Dr. Bhenke spent a week with us and it was a great association.

After our chamber was completed and functional, the Virginia Mason hospital physicians became interested in its use for hyperbaric medical treatments. It was use for the treatment of gas gangrene, CO poisoning and a host of other medical problems.

One morning, our administrative staff informed me that a Nursing School had asked for a tour of the Hyperbaric and Diving physiology research laboratory. It was a nursing program from Everett Community College and they wanted to know if I was available to conduct the tour. They said that there would be about 20 students accompanied by the director of the nursing program. **Everett community college nursing program…** hmmm, yes I was available. I wouldn't have missed this opportunity for the world!

When the nursing students arrived. Our administrator introduced me to the group and beyond my every expectation, she included our breakthrough research in submarine medicine, and she cited four publications in the national literature that I had authored. The temptation to begin my presentation with the fact that I was an Everett Nursing Program dropout was overwhelming, but discretion being the better part of valor, I did not even mention my past association with the program.

I conducted a professional tour the facility answering complex medical questions about the research, but I never missed an opportunity to explain in depth, physiological processes in diving that went far beyond general medical knowledge, a fault of the ego, I admit, but one I was willing to accept.

When the tour was over, the nursing school director came up to me and said that she was very proud of me and that she wished that I could have completed the nursing program. I always thought that she was a great lady, and I told her that I had learned a lot from the training I got in the nursing classes. I also told her that I had accomplished what I wanted to do and that all my experiences in her program and at Everett General hospital had helped me in various ways to achieve that goal. She shook my hand, then she gave me a hug, and thanked me for the tour. I told her that she was welcome to bring groups from her program to the research center at any time.

The following months at the research center were filled with interesting and challenging research and diving adventures. Trips to Sea-life Park in Hawaii to work with the Dolphins and other large marine mammals, diving in the Bahamas and a visit to the Hydro Lab underwater habitat with my friend and one of my best assistant instructors Ben Barrie. We conducted undersea habitat programs in the Puget Sound. I got to attend Diving physiology symposiums around the United States and a couple of foreign countries. I did Speaking engagements, and scientific lectures for various professional groups. My personal research work and duties as the Northwest Regional training director for the National Association of Underwater Instructors kept me working in the areas that I loved. My involvement with the sport diving community of the Northwest kept me in good physical condition requiring several training dives or sport dives every week. With all these activities, life's time literally flew by, providing the continuous supply of learning experiences and adventures.

DIVING PHYSIOLOGY SYMPOSIUM
"MAN IN THE SEA" SEATTLE

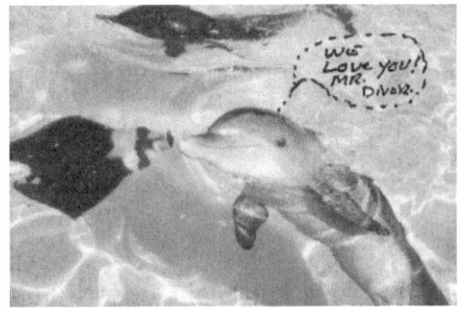

DIVING RESEARCH WITH THE
BOTTLE NOSE DOLPHINS AT SEA
LIFE PARK IN HAWAII

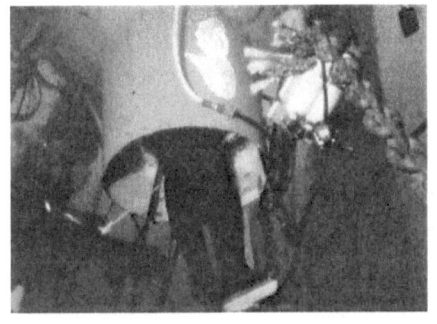

"MAN IN THE SOUND"
UNDERSEA STATION PROJECT.
DIVER ENTERING THE STATION

"HYDRO LAB" UNDERSEA STATION
IN THE BAHAMAS.

CHAPTER 18
ADVENTURE OF A LIFETIME

The biggest adventure of my life began in the spring of 1968 when Virginia Mason research center was asked to participate in the underwater exploration of the Cobb Seamount. This was an undersea mountain that lies approximately 270 nautical miles west of the Washington coast. It rises from a ten-thousand foot abyssal ocean plain and comes to within 120 feet of the surface of the Pacific Ocean.

A national Consortium of government agencies and academic institutions were formed and became sponsors of the research expeditions. The name of the project was "Sea Use." A few of the many participants were the University of Washington, University of Hawaii, University of Alaska, The U.S. Navy, The US Coast Guard, NOAA. The Honeywell Corp., The Oceanographic Institute of Washington and many others

The undersea mountain was a unique piece of underwater real estate. Just 270 nautical miles off the west coast of the United States, it held the interest of Oceanographers, Marine biologists and certain government agencies concerned with our national security. Initially, Project Sea Use envisioned turning the Cobb Seamount into an undersea laboratory by developing an underwater station on the mountain. Scientific and engineering divers would live and work on the undersea mountain. The concept was to make the Cobb Seamount the first permanent international undersea station.

What Project Sea Use proposed to do first, was to mount several exploratory diving expeditions to the seamount to study the feasibility of the project. When I was at the planning meetings as a representative of Virginia Mason Research Center, I asked the Sea-Use representatives where they proposed getting their diving team for the seamount expeditions?

Jon Lindbergh, who had been appointed to the council addressed me and said, "We were hoping we could rely on Virginia Mason Research Center and you for support in that area. Spence, we know that you do a lot of advanced Scuba diving training and we would like you to evaluate, select and train the diving team that will participate in the first Sea Use mission to the Cobb Seamount. You would go on the mission as the diving supervisor."

Now I got exited! The prospects of participating in such an exciting adventure, was beyond my wildest expectation. I started to accept the offer when it dawned on me that I could not participate unless Virginia Mason Research Center authorized it.
I looked across the table at Dr. Spencer in anticipation! Dr. Spencer leaned back in his chair and studied the situation for a few moments then he replied, "I believe we can volunteer Spence's service to participate in the project. It will give us an opportunity to study the physiological stress and decompression results on SCUBA diving in the open ocean." Brilliant! I would have never thought of a good enough reason to involve VMRC in the project but because of the

depth of the dives at the seamount, they would all require decompression on all the dives My mind was racing over the prospects of leading the diving on such an adventure!

The project was now a reality and throughout the spring months, we conducted number of planning meetings and team training sessions. Various agencies and academic institutions submitted scientist and engineers to be considered for the first Sea Use Diving Team. All the candidates selected were subjected to a rigorous medical exam.

The divers selected were required to attend classes on the history of the seamount. Since its discovery in 1950, there had been a couple of oceanographic expeditions to the mountain by the University of Washington and Oregon State University. Two divers from the University of Washington made a descent to the pinnacle. The dive time was limited and the rough sea conditions made diving in SCUBA gear hazardous. Because of the short duration of the dives, only a small amount of data was gathered by those divers.

In 1965, Oregon State University made several trips to the Cobb Seamount and developed a research project. The project would attempt to anchor an instrument mast to the top pf the Seamount; which would transmit both oceanographic and weather data to the mainland. Several dives by university divers were made to the pinnacle during this project. The dives were conducted under the direction of Jim Washburn, diving officer for the university. Unfortunately, the project was doomed as the sea became very rough and destroyed the mast when it's anchoring had nearly been completed.

Although I didn't know Jim Washburn, I thought that his previous diving experience at the Cobb Seamount would be invaluable and I contacted Jim and invited him to participate in the Sea Use expedition. The first Sea Use mission to the seamount was scheduled for August 1968 and he could not escape a previous commitment. He was very helpful and agreed to come to the research center and give us information on the diving conditions and recommendations he had for our diving team.

The months of May, June and July were filled with meetings and planning sessions. Training was scheduled for the divers who would be selected for the first mission to the seamount. The Sea Use Council was receiving requests from the scientific community to participate in the mission with their scientific projects.

All divers being considered for this mission had to submit their diving credentials, diving history, and a brief synopsis of the scientific project that they would conduct at the Seamount. The divers were then chosen by the council and I was notified to review their qualifications and that I would have the final say as to whether the diver would be accepted on the team.

The real final acceptance would be if they passed the training regimen that I had developed for this first team of Project Sea Use. To qualify for the team, the divers had to take an extensive written examination on Diving Physics and Physiology, diving equipment and decompression procedures.

They were given a map of the pinnacle of Cobb Seamount that showed the approximate location of several scientific instruments that were placed on the mountain during past non-diving expeditions. They were also given pictures of the equipment that they would be searching for as one of the projects on this mission. They were told to study the map and pictures of the instruments and then tested on their knowledge of the material.

The instruments were designed to gather a variety of oceanographic and ecological data and were to be retrieved after several months on the Seamount. Floating buoys were tethered to the instruments so that they could be found and recovered, however, all the buoys were lost in the fierce winter storms that ravage the North Pacific and if any equipment could be recovered it would have to be by divers.

The two main purposes of the first mission were first, to search for and recover as many of the instrument packages as possible and second, to explore the pinnacle of the seamount and a plateau at 150 feet. Exploration of the plateau would provide information for the potential development of the seamount as the site of a permanent offshore undersea station.

In the first two months of the project, I gathered all the information that was available from any dives at the seamount that were recorded by previous expeditions. About two weeks later, Jim Washburn, the Diving Officer from Oregon State University came to visit me at VMRC. He was a stocky built man with a warm friendly personality. Jim and I hit it off immediately.

When we finished touring the VMRC facility, we discussed the first Sea Use mission to the Cobb Seamount and Jim gave me some drawings that he had made of the approximate location of the anchors that were used on the ill-fated Totem Project. He described the diving environment in detail and cautioned that all the divers we intended to take on the mission should be very strong physically, and very well trained as divers! We talked through most of the morning and I made lots of notes.

I told Jim that I would like him to come with us on the mission as a diving officer. He said he would love to go, but he had an important commitment that wouldn't allow him to get away. I told him that if in the future I was the Diving Supervisor, he was welcome on any of the subsequent missions.

Jim and I spent the rest of the day going over diving operations. We developed a great rapport. Jim was a great guy, and I was disappointed that he wouldn't be with us on this first Sea Use mission. The weeks passed and the final dive team was selected for the mission. It was exciting to realize that we were going to explore an undersea mountain inaccessible to all but skilled divers and more mysterious than the surface of the moon.

Carl Ulrich, our diving lab technician and second class navy diver would be one of our diving officers. Roland White, a student in the Scientific and Engineering Program at Bellevue Community College and my most experienced teaching assistant would also serve as a diving officer. Four other students from the diving program at the college were chosen to participate as team divers and four divers from the Honeywell Marine Systems Center would make up the remainder of the team.

In addition to the divers, the scientific head of the expedition would be Dr. Robert Burns, head of the school of Oceanography at the University of Washington. Our diving medical officer would be Dr. Merrill Spencer our Director of VMRC. We would have a decompression chamber and the trained medical personnel to treat any potential decompression sickness. This would always be a danger when diving to depths over 100 feet.

The Sea Use foundation had secured the support of the ESSA prime research ship the Oceanographer. This was a large ship, specially equipped for open ocean research. During the last week of preparation, we loaded all our diving equipment aboard, set up our decompression chamber and conducted emergency drills with our divers and the ship's crew.

The day before we were to leave we were conducting some diver staging operations, lowering the divers off the ship to the water and then retrieving them back to the deck of the ship. I was supervising the operation when the ships loudspeaker announced that I had a phone call. It was Overlake Hospital informing me that my youngest son Scott had been hit by a car and was in their emergency room! I turned the diving operation over to my assistant supervisor and set a speed record for getting from Lake Union to Bellevue and into the hospital emergency room! I feared the worst, and I was totally relieved when the attending physician informed me that Scott had just been grazed by the car and knocked off his bicycle. He was a little shook up, but otherwise not seriously hurt. Susan and I were so thankful that a few seconds separated him from a fatal injury. We could take him home within a few hours.

    We spent a quiet evening at home eternally thankful that our son wasn't seriously injured. I spent most of the evening with Susan and my two sons Ron and Scott, grateful that the family was intact. Scot had been spared serious injury by the grace of God. Before I retired for the night, I packed a suitcase with clothes and personal belongings for the trip. I didn't sleep very well that night and I dreamt about diving.

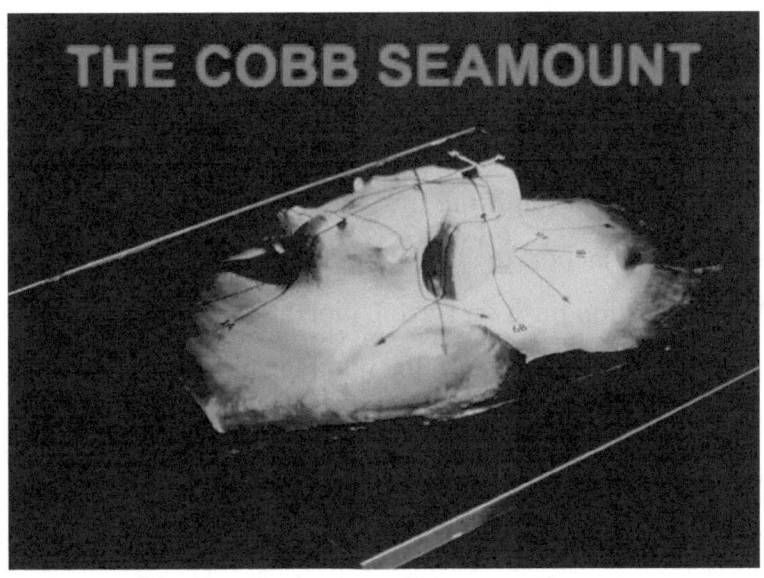

CHAPTER 19
SEA USE MISSION ONE

I was up around 5:00 AM and had to be at the ship by 7:00. Our sailing time was 8:00 AM and I wanted to be there early to check on my divers and do a last-minute check on our equipment. I said my goodbyes to Susan and the boys and left the house about 5:45. I got to the ship around 6:30 and was relieved to see that most of the diving crew was arriving at about the same time. By 7:30, the diving crew was aboard and the equipment check was complete.

Dr. Robert Burns, our chief scientist and Dr. Spencer arrived around 7:15. As soon as they were aboard, Dr. Burns called a short meeting of the Sea Use team to discuss conduct aboard the ship and preparations for sailing. After the final briefing, Last minute preparations, and a warning from the ship's loud speaker that the ship was weighing anchor, the Oceanographer slipped from her Pacific Marine Station birth on Lake Union and made her way through the Ballard Locks and up the main channels of the Puget Sound to the Straits of Juan De Fuca.

While we were in relatively quiet waters, our diving team and the ship's crew checked and double-checked all our equipment to see that it was secured for sea. Once we hit the Pacific Ocean at Cape Flattery we could potentially encounter some rough ocean conditions: although no rough weather was predicted for the foreseeable future.

After a smooth sail through the straits of Juan de Fuca we passed Cape Flattery and out into the vast waters of the Pacific Ocean. The ship was making about 20 knots as we watched the shoreline and the mountain ranges of the Olympics and Vancouver Island slowly sink below the horizon and we could experience the curvature of the earth. Other than being in a high-altitude aircraft or spaceship, the calm waters of the open ocean is one of the only places on the surface of the planet where you can get a real feel of our earth as a sphere.

As we sailed through the morning and into the afternoon, the sea lost its' grey-green hue and began to take on a darker blue-green appearance. Later in the afternoon, we could no longer see the mainland and the ship plowed her way toward the great expanse of water and to our rendezvous with the Cobb Seamount.

Several of the diving team joined me as we stood out on deck and watched as our ship chased the red-orange orb of the setting sun sinking quickly below the western horizon. In what seemed like but a few moments, we lost the race and the last sliver of golden sun slipped below the sea, leaving the western sky ablaze with flaming crimson tongues and the silhouettes of high white clouds.

As twilight fell, the cool breeze of the salt air tinged the nostrils and set off a feeling in my body that somehow I was one with the sea. Since over 70% of our bodies are basically salt water, perhaps that feeling is the nature of our being. Even though this was my first major sea voyage; I felt as if I had been here many times before. It all seemed familiar to me and the feeling gave me the peace and satisfaction one gets when returning home after a long journey!

After dinner and some conversations with my diving officers, I went to the cabin I was sharing with Dr. Burns. The sea was relatively calm and the ship was running smoothly. When I closed my eyes, I could visualize the sharp white bow of the Oceanographer slicing through the blue-green water. Within moments, the gentle roll of the ship became anesthetic and I drifted into a fitful sleep.

Dr. Burns called to me about 5:30 in the morning and I responded by rolling out of my bunk. As my feet touched the deck I stood up to find that there was more roll and pitching motion from the ship. The water was somewhat more active as we sailed farther out into the Pacific Ocean.

After breakfast, I went out on deck to the diving staging area. Roland was already there checking on the diving equipment. I spoke to him for a few minutes and he informed me that some of the divers were a bit queasy from the ship motion. That was to be expected in the first few days at sea. The divers could take seasick medicine like Dramamine, but they could not dive until they were off the medication for at least 24 hours. When I finished my briefing with Roland, I walked to the fantail of the ship and looked out at the wake of the ship as steamed toward the Cobb Seamount.

The sun was rising in the east and there was no sight of land. We were now over 200 miles at sea and as the sun rose steadily in the morning sky I could see that the blue-green water of yesterday was now a deep azure blue. I understand that the deep blue color of the pelagic ocean is due to Hydrogen, but whatever causes it, the deep blue color of the ocean meant very clear water, and was good news for diving operations.

Several of the diving team had started to gather on deck and I was walking back to the diving station area when Roland called to me and pointed out off the forward quarter of the ship. My first impression was that the beautiful blue water was dotted with hundreds of miniature white sailboats. They were the floating bladders of a pelagic jellyfish. There were literally thousands of them and for about 10 nautical miles, we sailed through a huge band of tiny white jellyfish.

Now it was down to business. When most of the diving team had assembled on deck, we conducted some training on the decompression chamber and did more tests on the diving equipment. We had a team briefing and posted the diving roster for the order of the dives. It was easy to see that the team was excited about diving on the undersea mountain and possibly a little intimidated by the vastness and conditions of the open ocean.

Around 1:30 in the afternoon word came down from the bridge that we were nearing the Seamount. Precise satellite navigation had put the ship within a couple of miles of the pinnacle of the Seamount. All the expedition members were on deck to see the Oceanographer maneuver toward the pinnacle and although all we could see were ocean swells, we knew that the ship was now hovering above the steep slopes of the undersea mountain.

The mountain was situated on an abyssal ocean plain and rose from a depth of 10,000 feet to within 120 feet of the surface. If one could stand on the ocean floor and look at the mountain from a distance, it would somewhat resemble Mt. Rainier. Instead of the Cascade Range of mountains that is home to Mt. Rainier, Cobb Seamount is part of the Cascadia range of undersea mountains. One of the divers commented that we were about to start mountain climbing from the top down.

As the Oceanographer searched for the pinnacle, we could see a large flock of sea birds off in the distance. In the wind, I could detect the faint odor of what smelled like tide flats and a passage from "Moby Dick" entered my mind. *"When ye smell land where there is no land*!" Well, I could smell land and I figured that we were either very near the pinnacle of Cobb Seamount; or were about to be attacked by a big white whale!

As the ship moved slowly toward the pinnacle, one of the ships' crew pointed out a reddish object floating in the water. When we got closer we could see that it was a cylindrical red buoy that appeared to be anchored to the top of the mountain. We were surprised and intrigued by the red buoy and since there had been no known recent expeditions to the mountain, we were curious to know how it got there!

The Oceanographer sailed slowly around the undersea mountain to get a feel for the size and shape of the shallow pinnacle. When the ships' Fathometer had traced a pretty good picture of the top of the mountain, members of the ship's crew scurried to the fantail and prepared to drop an anchor and a large temporary buoy that would mark the shallowest part of the pinnacle. After a few minutes of slow maneuvering, the anchor was dropped and the brightly colored orange buoy marked the top of the undersea mountain. The Oceanographer would now be able to maintain a good visual reference while holding station on the pinnacle.

When the big ship eased away from the marker buoy, we could look over the side and see the top of the pinnacle 130 feet below. You couldn't make out details, but you could see a definite reflection off the bottom and as the ship drifted over the edge of the pinnacle, the whitish color of the bottom abruptly turned to the deep blue of the abyssal depths. All the divers were staring down over the side of the ship and remarking about the clarity of the water. The event of reaching the Seamount stimulated their excitement for their first dive to the mountain.

It was about 3:00 in the afternoon when we finally got the Oceanographer situated on station. After a short meeting with Dr. Burns and the Captain of the ship, we decided to wait till the next morning to start diving operations. During the rest of the afternoon, we speculated about the buoy that we had seen when we first reached the pinnacle. We were close enough to the buoy at one time that we could see Canadian markings. We assumed that it had been dropped there by a Canadian, oceanographic research vessel. The question was whether it was just a buoy marking the pinnacle or whether it was anchored to some structure or instrument. It was decided that the first dive would be to see what was on the bottom beneath the buoy.

After a meeting with Dr. Burns, the ships operations officer and the diving team, we conducted some emergency decompression treatment drills. The diving officers and I set up the diving roster and assigned two-man diving teams for each of the planned tasks.

Roland White and I would make the first dive. I wanted to see what the diving environment was like, and to be honest, I wanted to see the mountain. Roland was a good underwater photographer and we wanted pictures of whatever was down there! Rolland was also one of the best divers on my team and I liked having him as my diving buddy, particularly on a dive like this one.

With all the planning meetings and training drills over, Roland and I carefully checked our diving gear for our morning dive. We were both excited and speculated as to what the dive might hold in store for us. The sea state had been calm with long rolling swells and we hoped it would stay that calm for tomorrow's dive.

After the evening meal, Roland and I went out on deck and watched the last rays of sunlight fade over the horizon. One hundred and forty feet below the ship was the top of a gigantic undersea mountain; unseen and undetected by man until a couple of decades ago! Only a couple of divers from Oregon State University and the University of Washington have ever visited the top of this sunken volcanic mountain and only for a few minutes. The Cobb Seamount was a unique geologic wonder and her secrets were still waiting for discovery. I felt exhilarated and privileged to get to experience the true meaning of exploration!

ARTIST DRAWING OF THE CONCEPT OF THE SEA USE PROGRAM GOAL OF DEVELOPING A FIRST PERMANENT UNDERSEA STATION ON THE COBB SEAMOUNT.

CHAPTER 20
WELCOME TO COBB SEAMOUNT

I don't know about Roland, but with the anticipation of that first dive to the mountain, it was a little difficult to get to sleep. Finally, I drifted off and slept soundly until the morning wake up call. I washed up and dressed quickly then I went to the mess deck to meet Roland. Neither of us was very interested in a big breakfast, there was just too much excitement and we both knew we would have to tolerate a few hours of rocking and rolling while we operated out of the small rubber Zodiac boat.

About an hour and a half later, the ship was ready. The diving team was at their stations, and Roland and I stood on the deck in full dive gear with twin tanks. All our dives to the mountain would require decompression stops at 20ft. and 10 ft. Our average depth would be about 130. At that depth, a single tank of air could be depleted very rapidly if heavy exertion or some emergency would cause the diver's breathing rate to increase dramatically. All the seamount dives would be conducted using twin tanks to provide a safe amount of air. This would give our divers sufficient air to complete their dives and safely return to the decompression stops. An additional air supply source would be available for the divers on the decompression stops.

When the Zodiac boat had been launched with our topside diving support crew, the Oceanographer moved into position next to red buoy that we found floating atop the pinnacle. Roland and I mounted a stage which raised us over the side and lowered us to the water, where we could make a short surface swim over to the buoy and our Zodiac boat. As soon as we were safely alongside our safety boat, the Oceanographer moved away from the diving station and stood by at a safe distance of 50 to 100 yards.

The sea swells were about 4 to 6 feet, gentle and steady. As we bobbed up and down in the swells we lost sight of the Oceanographer when we were at the bottom of the swell. If we looked anywhere but at the Zodiac boat, there was nothing except ocean. After observing the vastness of the sea for a moment, I looked at Roland and uttered a modified version of a very famous line. *"Oh God, thy Sea is so great and we are so small!"* He nodded his head in agreement!

We synchronized our time with the topside crew and prepared to descend the buoy line. It seemed strange that we were descending to the top of a mountain. Roland and I set our bottom timers and underwater watches and on cue, we placed our regulators in our mouths and started our decent to the Cobb Seamount. The water was deep blue and the visibility was well over 100 feet. We looked down and we could see the surface of the pinnacle. There were irregular geometric like lines in the surface of the rock. The patterns were reticular, which was characteristic of a sunken volcanic mountain.

When we were within 30 feet of the pinnacle, we were surrounded by huge schools of rockfish. Some of the fish were large red snapper and there must have been $20,000 worth of fish fillets swimming around us! Roland was our official underwater photographer and he immediately started taking pictures of me, and everything around us. When we had descended the line from the buoy, we could see that the anchor weight of the buoy was snagged on a wire line that trailed off down into a large crater of rock.

Roland and I checked our depth and bottom time. The depth was 130 feet. Our air pressures were good and our bottom time left for the dive was 18 minutes. If we were going to see where the wire leads, we would have to get moving. Our restrictions were that we could not exceed 150 feet and we must only go the point of no return which meant we must be able to get back to the line ascending from the bottom to the buoy before our bottom time ran out! The ascending line led up to our decompression station where we would be required to take some mandatory stops at 20 feet and 10 feet below the surface. Without adequate decompression from our dive, we would risk getting the "Bends".

The wire line was leading off into the distance and disappeared over a ledge of rock, then down into deeper water. I motioned to Roland and I started following the wire with Roland alongside snapping pictures. The wire led us down a small incline and then slightly up a small ridge. At the bottom of the incline, our depth gauges read 140 feet. As we approached the edge of the ridge, I estimated that we had traveled about sixty yards from the descending line. Just over the ridge, the bottom dropped down over some ledges into a large crater.

For a moment, I was startled! There, about 60 feet away was a huge, long cylinder about 5 to 6 feet in diameter and about 40 feet long! From our position we couldn't make out what it was. I looked at Roland and his eyes, told me he was surprised too! It was too large to be one of the instruments we were looking for. Could it be some sort of construction? Could some foreign country have placed some sort of habitat or station on the Cobb Seamount? I was beginning to get a little excited! I checked my watch and we had only about 12 minutes left on the dive. I motioned to Roland and we quickly moved toward the cylinder. As we reached it, both Roland and I knew what we had found. It was the remains of the bottom half of the Oregon State University's Totem mast. The ill-fated mast was destroyed by the huge seas which came up during the attempt to anchor it!

Roland and I surveyed the remains of the mast. What we found amazing was that the three-quarter inch steel cylinder had been ripped in half by the raging sea! The torn and jagged midsection of the mast was a visual testimony to the destructive power of the ocean! Roland and I looked at the damage, then at each other and we both shook our heads. Roland took pictures of the cylinder from all angles and we both posed for pictures.

While Roland was taking the last picture of me with the mast, a yellow caution light flashed in my mind. I looked at the depth gauge. It read 148 feet and we had only six minutes left to swim about 60 yards back to the poly line leading up to our decompression station! I motioned to Roland, pointed to my watch and then to the wire line. He got the message immediately!

As Roland and I swam briskly back along the bottom, I realized that the slight narcotic effect of the depth and fixation on our discovery could have easily caused us to exceed our bottom time. This would have required us to take more decompression than planned. Since I was the one who specified the limits on the team's decompression times, I didn't want to be the one who violated them! We arrived at the buoy line with about one minute left of our maximum bottom time. With a few seconds to go, Roland and I started up the line carefully controlling our ascent rate.

As we ascended about 50 feet we could look up and see the bottom of the Zodiac boat silhouetted against the rolling surface. At 40 feet, we moved off the ascent line and swam over to the decompression line and our extra air supply if it was needed. Our decompression was monitored by our topside crew and they gave us signals when we were to leave each stop and when to surface. While Roland and I were hanging off on the decompression stops, we experienced a gentle rolling motion as we both stared out into the azure blue infinity of ocean. Our senses were now sharp in the absence of the narcotic effect that we experienced at depth. In a few minutes, we finished our decompression and surfaced to the Zodiac boat and we were taken aboard.

The Zodiac boat was untied from the Canadian buoy and our topside crew radioed the Oceanographer that they were bringing the divers back to the ship. When we got alongside he Oceanographer, the ship's crew had lowered a stage platform into the water. Roland and I rolled off the Zodiac boat, swam the short distance and boarded the diver's stage for the ride up to the main deck.

Roland and I debriefed with Dr. Burns and our diving officers. We told them that we had found remains of the Totem mast in a small crater at 150 feet. Roland produced the roll of film he had taken on the dive and since the film could be developed aboard the ship, we would soon have photographic proof of our find. Everyone was excited at our discovery of the Totem Mast as it promoted optimism for finding the lost instrument packages. If the sea state would cooperate, we would start search dives this afternoon. Roland and I briefed the next two dive teams on the conditions and warned them that they had to stay focused on their depth and bottom time

It was about 12:30 when the crew had completed launching a small tender boat that we would use to tow the diving teams across the pinnacle on a trapeze bar towing system while looking for the lost instruments. The divers would be using twin aluminum 90 cubic foot tanks filled with a 50%/50% nitrogen-oxygen gas mixture.

If they were to use air as a breathing medium, they would be restricted to a total of 30 minutes at 90 feet before entering the decompression zone. If they exceeded 25 minutes they would be obligated to take decompression stops before coming to the surface. The 50/50 gas mixture would allow them to stay underwater for 25 minutes on the towing bar; surface and take a short ten-minute break and then descend again to 90 feet for another 30 minutes. This would double the time they could safely spend at 90 feet if they were breathing compressed air.

From the trapeze bar, the divers could easily see the bottom which was an average of 40 feet below them. With the excellent visibility, and both divers scanning for instrument packages, they could observe a lot of area as they were towed around over the pinnacle. The towing boat was receiving instructions by radio to steer a course defined by equipment aboard the Oceanographer. An engineer aboard the ship could chart the area of the pinnacle covered by the divers. When one team of divers finished their dives, our rubber Zodiac boat would shuttle them back to the Oceanographer and deliver a new team of divers to the towing boat.

We ran three teams of towed divers that first day plus the dive Roland and I had made in the morning. Even though the towed searching system was very effective, no instruments were found. One team did locate one of the large anchors used for the Totem mast project of the Oregon state university. Two of the teams reported seeing sharks, mostly small *"oceanic blues"* Another team said they saw two big white tips sharks milling around the Zodiac boat as they started their dive. Aside the spotting of sharks the diving went as planned.

The first diving day of project Sea Use was over. All the divers were safely aboard the Oceanographer. At our team debriefing meeting, more pictures of the pinnacle were passed around among the Sea Use divers for orientation to the environment that they were about to experience on subsequent dives to the Seamount.

After dinner and before going to bed, I checked the diving team rotation for the next day. Carl Eurich and I were scheduled to make the second dive on the towed search and I went to bed with the anticipation of another visit to the Cobb Seamount. Everything seemed well and the diving seemed too easy so far. Little did I know that the situation was about to change.

The next morning our towed dives went without a hitch. Carl and I made the second dive and riding on the tow bar was great. We kept expecting to find something, but all we saw was interesting formations of large pillow lava and lots of Cobb Seamount pinnacle. The dive team before us located another of the large anchors used on the Totem project, but no instrument packages were found. We speculated that they were possibly dragged off the mountain top by foreign trawlers. There was evidence that both the Japanese and Russians had fished the seamount.

The morning towed dives were completed and it was decided that we would conduct another dive at the oceanographic buoy. We elected to make this dive in light weight, line tended diving gear with an emergency SCUBA back up system (called a bail out system) The divers were Jim Gavin and Chuck Blackstock, Engineers from Honeywell Inc.

After spending about ten minutes on the bottom, the divers had trouble breathing from the surface supplied system. During the descent, the diver's emergency regulators became entangled in their line tended harnesses and there was a significant delay as the divers tried to access their emergency bail out systems. This resulted in both divers making a rapid ascent to the surface. The divers were immediately recovered and brought safely back aboard the ship. Shortly after we got them aboard, Jim began to show symptoms of the bends and had to be treated in the decompression chamber.

The recompression treatment appeared to be successful, but the ship was beyond helicopter range should Jim require more serious medical attention. On the recommendation of Dr. Spencer; who was serving as our Submarine Medical Physician, the rest of the mission was aborted and the Oceanographer set sail for Seattle. It was a big disappointment to the diving team not to finish the mission, but safety of the divers had to come first.

During the return trip to Seattle, I investigated, trying to determine the reason for the diving accident. I wanted to know why the divers lost air from the surface supplied system. Apparently, the pressure to the divers had been erroneously adjusted by one of our divers from the specified settings resulting in an inadequate pressure to supply the diving apparatus for both divers at their operating depth. My team had nearly made a fatal error and because I was the diving supervisor, I accepted the error as mine. In retrospect, I saw ways in which I could have safeguarded against the problem. It was another harsh lesson in the critical world of diving!

DRAWING BY VINCE RAINIER OF DIVERS BEING TOWED AT 90 FEET OVER THE MOUNTAIN.

DIVERS ON THE TRAPEZE BAR AT 90 FEET BREATHING 50% NITROGEN AND 50% OXYGEN. SEARCHING FOR INSTRUMENTS PLACED ON THE PINNACLE OF THE MOUNTAIN

ROLAND WHITE, MY DIVING OFFICER AND TEAM DIVER TOOK THIS UNDERWATER PHOTO AT 140 FEET AS WE CAME UPON THE REMAINS OF THE OREGON STATE UNIVERSITY ILL FATED INSTRUMENT MAST.

CHAPTER 21
MISSION NUMBER TWO

About a month after the diving accident marred the Sea Use I mission, the Sea Use Council decided to plan another mission to the Cobb Seamount to take place the following year. The Sea Use Council requested that I serve on the second mission as Assistant Diving Supervisor. I would be working with Ret. Master Chief Robert Sheats, who was at that time living in Poulsbo, Washington. Bob Sheats was one of the navy's most famous Master divers. He was a prisoner of war during the Second World War, and suffered the brutality of the famous Bataan death march. He was one of the navy's senior Master Divers and served on many experimental missions such as the Navy Sea lab experiments.

The council said that Chief Sheats was willing to volunteer his time to assist us in planning, training, and conducting the mission. I realized that because of his vast experience in supervising diving operations that we would be lucky to have him guide us through this next mission. I would be able to learn a lot from him.

During the next few months we continued research work at VMRC and in February, the Sea Use Council began a series of planning meetings for project Sea Use II. I spent some time in the previous months researching background on Chief Bob Sheats. He had an impeccable naval record and was truly one of our war heroes. From what I learned, he would be critical and demanding of our diving team. At our first meeting, he asked a lot of questions about my diving training and experience. His initial attitude was rather gruff and direct as if he didn't trust anyone who was not navy trained and qualified.

When he found out that I had graduated from commercial deep sea diving school, and that my instructor was retired navy Master Diver Eugene Mogus, his attitude softened somewhat. He was interested to learn about my diving experience on the hydroelectric dams, and was surprised that I had worked as a diver with Walter O'Shell, who after going to officer candidate school became a staff officer at the naval deep sea diving school.

The chief knew that I didn't have a lot of experience in the open ocean, or aboard large ships and he sort of took me under his wing and introduced me to the finer points of running diving operations from large ships. The chief was a great teacher, and I became a dedicated student. He taught me how to analyze the diving operation for hidden dangers and how to hold my ground when there was any conflict between the mission objectives and the safety of the divers. I remember him telling me "This is not war! There is no objective in this mission worth losing a life over!" He was right! He also taught me that misplaced enthusiasm and over eagerness can compromise safety.

The chief was great to work with, and instead of dismissing our techniques for team operations and scuba gear on the seamount, he liked the "*Free Ranging*" search technique Roland and I had developed for the team. The chief and I chose divers for the Sea Use

II mission and within a month we began training. Training consisted of Classroom work, testing, physical fitness, medical exam, nitrogen tolerance test to 200 feet on air in the chamber, and open water deep dive training. The chief spent a lot of time and got to know every diver on the team very well.

Shortly after our return from Sea Use I, I received a call from Vince Rainier. Vince was young boy of 14 when he assisted me teaching scuba diving at the Spokane YMCA. Vince was a very special person and I lost track of him when I left Spokane. Several years ago, someone told me that Vince had distinguished himself in high school football, but that was the last I heard about him.

Vince was now married with two children. He was working for the Boeing Company as a mechanical illustrator and had seen me on local TV with Dr. Dixie Lee Ray, who was at that time the director of the Pacific Science Center in Seattle. Years later she would become governor of the state of Washington. Dr. Ray and I had become great friends and she invited me on her show *"The Arches of Science"* several times to talk about diving physiology research and the underwater exploration of the Cobb Seamount.

It was great to hear from Vince and I invited him to come to the research center to see what we were doing. After several visits to the center and a couple of visits to Vince's home, we re-established our relationship. I offered Vince the opportunity to participate in the Cobb Seamount diving expeditions.

It didn't take long for Vince to hone his diving skills and meet all the requirements for the Sea Use mission II team. He was a husky good-looking guy with a quick wit and a keen sense of humor. Some of his flippant, offhand remarks gave you the impression that he was a wise guy; but once you got to know him, Vince was just Vince. He was very talented and very quick to learn. He had a natural ability for anything mechanical and he was very good with people. He was also big and strong and though he had a friendly nature, you inherently knew didn't want to make Vince mad! Chief Sheats took an immediate liking to Vince and, soon Vince became a respected member of the diving team.

    The training for Sea Use II was demanding! It included a three-quarter mile run along the beach in a wet suit and weight belt. We also carried all the other diving equipment except the tanks. The three-quarter mile run ended at a section of the beach where the team rapidly donned their twin tanks and swam back along the shoreline to the starting point. This exercise was conducted after the regular morning physical fitness and diving drills. Emergency drills were conducted for the recovery of an unconscious diver. Each member of the diving team was required to bring a diver in full gear and twin tanks up from 20 feet. Then, strip off both the victims and their own diving gear and get the unconscious diver into a small rubber Zodiac boat with the assistance of the Zodiac crew.

    Through Nitrogen Tolerance Testing in the chamber, every team member had to become qualified to dive compressed air to 200 feet. They were trained to operate the decompression chamber and be familiar with the treatment tables. By July, only weeks before the Sea Use II mission, the diving team was physically fit and ready.

The Training was demanding, and some candidates from other diving research programs failed to qualify. Vince was selected to participate in the Sea Use II mission. We trained 16 divers and picked 10 to go on the mission. The chief and I along with the 10 divers and our diving team doctor would make up the Sea Use II diving team. Jim Washburn from Oregon State University would be joining us this time as part of the team.

CHAPTER 22
SEAMOUNT WITH THE COAST GUARD

This mission to the Cobb Seamount would be staged out of Astoria Oregon (where I had finished my river swim). For 12 days, we would be the live aboard guests of the United States Coast guard. We would be sailing to the seamount aboard the Ivy a 180 foot WLB class buoy tender with a crew that routinely conducts buoy and navigation aid maintenance in the mouth of the Columbia and other Washington and Oregon bays and rivers.

The captain of the buoy tender Ivy would be commander Ransom Boyce. Commander Boyce was a graduate of the U.S. Coast Guard Academy. He had been a ship's engineering officer and he knew a lot about ships and engines. He was an excellent ship handler and knew a lot of Marlon spike seamanship, the art and science of knots, tackle and rigging. Commander Boyce's executive officer would be Lieutenant Brock. His engineering officer was Lieutenant Bernstein. Commander Boyce and Lieutenant Brock came to Seattle about two weeks before the mission was to start and attended a meeting with the Sea Use Council and some of Seamount personnel. Chief Sheats and I attended the meeting and the chief outlined our diving operation plan to Commander Boyce and Lt. Brock

During the two weeks before the mission, we were very busy packing, checking inventory, and staging the all the equipment that would be needed to supply the diving operations. When everything was loaded onto trucks and vans, we left Seattle and headed for Astoria and the start of the Sea Use II mission.

Our convoy of equipment and personnel arrived at the coast guard base in Astoria about 11:00 AM in the morning. The gate guards were expecting us and we could drive our trucks out onto the dock next to the coast guard cutter Ivy, the ship that would take us to the undersea mountain, Lieutenant Brock met us when we arrived and introduced us to Chief Bosun Mate known as Chief Mac. The chief was a man in his early fifties just a few years from retirement. He presented a gruff exterior and I got the distinct impression that he was not happy about having a bunch of civilians aboard his ship.

I thought maybe when he got to know Bob Sheats, a retired navy master chief, he would warm up to us a bit. Lieutenant Brock turned us over to Chief Mac and went back aboard the Ivy. The chief told us to off-load our trucks and vans, and some of his deck crew would help us load our gear on pallets to be transferred aboard the ship.

About two hours after we arrived at the dock, engineers from the Naval Civil Engineering Laboratory arrived with a small crew and a trailer carrying the huge explosive anchor that would be tested on the seamount. There were other instrument packages at the loading area supplied by the Honeywell Company, the Nereus Corp, and the Numec Corp. They were for gathering current and surge information. Those instruments would be deployed on this mission and recovered on a subsequent mission the following year. Along with the scientific packages, there were three prototype sonic beacons that would be used to relocate the instruments deployed on this mission. These beacons would be battery powered and they would test the beacon housing before using a nuclear power source on future missions.

As the deck crew helped us load our equipment, I sensed some skepticism and resentment. I didn't blame them much because we were an unknown entity that had been dropped into their world. I'm sure they felt like they would be babysitting us throughout the entire mission. When we took a break from loading our gear, I got the diving team together and explained my feelings about our relationship with the crew. Most of the divers on the team were trained in basic seamanship and shipboard protocol and I asked them to act like seamen and use correct nautical terminology. I told them to be respectful and try to learn from the crew.

Throughout the afternoon, we loaded our diving gear including a two-lock decompression chamber aboard the Ivy. Petty officers that ran various sections of the ship, helped us organize and stow equipment. Chief Mac was all over the ship, giving orders to various sections. He was a merciless to his deck crew and shouted orders and chewed their tails relentlessly. Later, we found out that this was a relatively new deck crew and the chief was trying to mold them into a safe and efficient team. The working deck of the coast guard buoy tender is a dangerous place for the best trained crews and no place for the careless or the undisciplined!

The Sea Use diving team needed a place to store wet suits and other diving gear as well as a place to dress into and out of our diving suits. We were given the paint locker for our diving area. This area was in the forecastle of the ship, a raised section on the bow of the ship with compartments for anchor chain and rigging gear used in buoy tending and shipboard operations. I put Vince in charge of converting the paint locker into a diving locker and to see that the diver's equipment was organized and stored properly. He was also to set up an area where our wet suits could be dried. Vince was working alongside most of the deck crew during the afternoon and was a constant witness to the chiefs' tyrannical control of the new seamen; who despite their best efforts never seem to be able to do anything well enough to suit the chief.

The chief gave the deck crew a break around 2:30 in the afternoon. Most of the men went into the new diving locker compartment to sit down for their break. They sat on various benches in the locker and started to relax. Now, Vince had the entire deck crew as a captive audience in the locker. Vince became Vince, and started mimicking Chief Mac to the deck crew. He stood with his back to the compartment hatch and delivered of a bunch of colorful directions, imitating the chiefs' voice and manner.

The deck crew howled with laughter as Vince called up as many of the chiefs' orders and colorful adjectives as he could remember. The more the crew laughed, the more Vince performed! Suddenly, in the middle of Vince's performance, all the laughter stopped abruptly and a look of shock and awe crept onto the crews' faces.

It was then that Vince felt the presence of someone standing in the hatch way directly behind him. He fell silent, and slowly turned around to see Chief Mac a few feet away staring at him with a menacing glare. Finally, after a long silence Chief Mac said, "I'll do the yelling around here!" when I heard about the incident, I told Vince, "thanks a lot Vince I'm sure you endeared yourself to the chief for the rest of the mission!" I think Vince felt bad about it at first, but he soon got over it because, Vince was Vince!

SEA USE DIVING TEAM TRAINING ABOARD A NAVY TUG.

LOADING THE COAST GUARD CUTTER AT PORT ASTORIA.

ENROUTE TO THE COBB SEAMOUNT WITH THE COAST GUARD.

THE COAST GUARD SHIP ON STATION AT THE COBB

Chapter 23
THE IVY TAKES US TO COBB

By late afternoon, the Ivy was loaded and all the Sea Use personnel were aboard. It was now time to assign the sleeping quarters for the Sea Use crew. The chief scientist on this mission was Dr. Walt Sands from the University of Washington Department of Oceanography. He and Ron Hoss, a representative of the Sea Use Council and a documentary filmmaker would share a state room in officer country. Chief Sheats and I would share a state room. Dr. Callison, our Submarine Medical Physician would bunk in the pharmacy in the corpsman's quarters. The rest of the team would fill empty bunks in the crew's quarters.

The chief asked me to assemble all the Sea Use crew below decks in the crew's quarters, so he could assign bunks, distribute bedding, and go over the ships rules and protocol. After he had finished assigning bunks and briefing the divers, He asked everyone to check their issue of bedding. "Does everyone have all of their bedding?" He asked. One of our young divers who shall remain nameless spoke up and exclaimed "Chief Mac, I don't seem to have a fitted mattress cover."

Now for those of you not familiar with military descriptions of common items like the mattress cover, let us say that a "fitted mattress cover" would be far too sophisticated a name for this item! All the experience divers in the team winced at the declaration. A

149

huge and diabolical grin crept onto the chiefs' face as he addressed our young diver in a most condescending voice. "**well, sweetie**," he said. "**I'll see to it that you get a fitted mattress cover**." We all wanted to die as we again succeeded in subtracting points from the chiefs' score sheet.

That evening, all the Sea Use crew got together in a local restaurant and had a "*bon voyage*" party. Again, everyone was reminded to try to be respectful of the military protocol and try to fit in with the crew. Except for the night watches, the crew retired around 10:30 PM. The night went fast and we were awakened with a typical shipboard reveille! As soon as I was dressed, I found Roland and Vince and told them that Chief Sheats wanted to have a meeting of the diving team right after breakfast.

Breakfast was also typical for the first day of sailing! It was chipped beef and gravy on toast, which was fondly referred to as something on a shingle. Sailing day breakfasts were diabolically designed by the cooks to be incompatible with the motion of the ship and I felt a little sorry for some of my team who had large second helpings!

Our morning meeting was over and we set about conducting last minute checks making sure everything was secured for the open sea. Captain Boyce arrived and after a final briefing with his officers, gave the orders to set sail. The deck crew retrieved the mooring lines and Captain Boyce backed the Ivy away from the dock and out into the Columbia River. It was a short trip down the river to the Columbia River bar and soon the Ivy was steaming out into the Pacific Ocean. It was a beautiful Sunday morning with the deep blue sky and a few puffy clouds The Columbia bar could be very rough at times and crossing it could easily initiate the day's epidemic of seasickness. Fortunately, the bar was calm that day and the crossing was kind to those new to ship motion.

The Ivy was 180 feet long with an icebreaker hull and she was rather narrow. Experienced Sailors aboard likened her ride to a navy destroyer, which does not have a reputation for comfort. Now the Ivy cut her way through the green water of the Washington coast and headed out to sea for our rendezvous with the Cobb Seamount. As we steamed out into the Pacific, the ship began to develop a gentle rolling and pitching motion. It was about two hours before the ocean started to claim victims.

By noon the epidemic has spread to the most susceptible. Fortunately, I was not one of them. I discovered two things that made me rather tolerant of the seasickness plague, food and Dramamine. I took some Dramamine before we left the dock at Astoria. I knew that I would feel a little grey and a lot relaxed. I just had to eat and get through the pitching motion while we were under way. That seemed to be the motion that affected me the most. The wallowing roll that we would have when they were on station, never seem to bother me, but would take its toll on some of the others.

I only needed the Dramamine to hold me for the first day of sailing and then I was great for the rest of the mission. The Dramamine was a big help, but a diver could not take Dramamine and dive because the medication would slow the diver's reactions and worsen the effects of nitrogen narcosis. Fortunately, most of the rest of the team handled the motion well.

Late that first afternoon, the crew targeted one of their new deck hands and set him up for "*mail buoy duty*". They said that a Coast Guard aircraft would drop a buoy containing a waterproof pouch with mail for the crew. He was dressed in full foul weather gear and a life jacket and they gave him a long pike pole with which to snag the mail pouch. They stationed him up on the point of the bow to get the mail when it was dropped. The crewmen bit hard, and sat attentively, waiting for a nonexistent mail buoy drop while the rest of the crew had a good laugh. After about two and a half hours of mail buoy duty, the novelty wore off, they let the seaman know he had been had!

The ocean swells were building steadily and the ride got a little rougher as the afternoon wore on. Some of the more resistant members of the crew succumbed to the motion and even a couple of a ship's officers were bitten by the seasickness bug. Everyone tries to tough it out and pretend that it doesn't affect them. Even the most experienced Sailors will confide that seasickness is no laughing matter and in extreme cases it could even have fatal consequences.

The ocean was now azure blue and small floating white jellyfish dotted the surface. The sun was setting in the west and the sky was crimson. Night was falling on the ocean and the Ivy switched on her running lights. The night was filled with a rhythmic pitching and rolling and sounds of the Ivy flexing her structure as she plowed through some of the larger swells. She was an aging matron among ships, but she was built strong and had a fine crew, and I felt safe aboard her.

Morning wake-up was piped into our cabin and Chief Sheats and I dressed and went to the mess hall for breakfast. The cooks had prepared a great breakfast of scrambled eggs and greasy sausages. The food was very good and there was plenty to eat, as there were only a few of us that were interested in eating! After breakfast, Chief Sheats got the diving team together and briefed everyone on our *"operation bends drill"* that we would conduct later that morning.

We had arranged with Captain Boyce and the crew to stop the ship so we could launch our rubber Zodiac boat and run a couple of drills. The drill would require us to launch the Zodiac boat with a four-man team. Three divers, dressed in wet suits and one fully dressed diver with twin tanks would man the boat. The team would position the Zodiac about 30 to 50 yards from the Ivy.

Our diver with the tanks would submerge below the Zodiac about 12 feet and then rise quickly to the surface. The drill would simulate an unconscious diver with the decompression sickness problem. The topside crew would have to haul the diver into the Zodiac, strip off his diving equipment as the Zodiac was speeding toward the Ivy. The diving team aboard the Ivy along with the deck crew would haul the injured diver from the Zodiac onto the Buoy Deck and then rapidly move him to the O2 deck where the decompression chamber team was waiting to start treatment.

153

After a rapid neurological exam by our submarine medicine physician, the diver would be taken into the decompression chamber with a member of the diving team to serve as an inside tender during the decompression treatment. We repeated the drill several times with various members of the team serving as the injured diver. We could complete the drill from the time the diver surfaced to the start of pressurization in the chamber in 3 minutes and 15 seconds.

After our practice sessions were over, the Ivy once again started steaming toward the undersea mountain. We were scheduled to arrive there around 3:00 in the afternoon. It would take more navigating skill to find the relatively small pinnacle of Cobb Seamount on this mission, because we did not have a satellite navigation system like we had on the ESSA ship Oceanographer. Captain Boyce and Lieutenant Brock were excellent navigators and with some good celestial navigation and the use of the UQN Fathometer, the Ivy worked her way over the submerge mountain toward the top.

The word was out that we were over the mountain and now searching for the pinnacle, so the Sea Use team went out on deck to see what they could see. I went up to the bridge and out onto the bridge wing. It wasn't long before I began to smell land, like tide flats but there was no land. There were quite a lot of sea birds in the area and I had noticed them last time we were at Cobb Seamount.

As the Ivy steamed slowly ahead, the quartermaster called the depth, "166 fathoms," about 1000 feet, "100 fathoms," 600 feet "50 fathoms," 300 feet. We were now over one of the shallow plateaus close to the top of the mountain. Lieutenant Brock had the quartermaster turned the ship a few degrees left and then the Fathometer started climbing rapidly, 50, 40, 30, 20 fathoms, then 30, 40 and 60 fathoms. We had just passed over the 120 foot pinnacle and sailed off the steep north face of the mountain.

After a couple of minutes, Captain Boyce gave a steering order and the Ivy executed a Williamson turn. A turn designed to bring the ship around 180 degrees to sail back over its previous track. It was used in 1943 by a naval captain by the name of Williamson to rescue a sailor by the name of Williamson who had fallen overboard. In this case, it was to relocate the 20-fathom area which would be the actual pinnacle of the undersea mountain.

Now Captain Boyce gave the order to make ready to drop a marker buoy on the pinnacle as the ship crosses the shallow area. He slowed the Ivy to about 3 to 5 knots forward speed and had a quartermaster call off the depth when we crossed the pinnacle. This time the small marker buoy was released in the middle of the 20-fathom area. Captain Boyce now had the deck crew ready a nine-ton concrete anchor block which they rigged over the side of the Ivy. To the anchor block they attached a mooring chain and a large black and white can buoy. This would serve to mark the pinnacle during our mission.

Using the Fathometer and a partially accurate chart of the pinnacle of Cobb Seamount, Captain Boyce and Lieutenant Brock worked the Ivy toward the east end of the 150-foot plateau. Once the Ivy was over the area, the deck crew deployed the anchor.

"Sploosh", went the huge concrete anchor, which the deck crew released by hitting a special kind of release lever with a sledgehammer. The release apparatus is called a *"pelican hook."*

The bright red painted concrete block plummeted down through the clear blue water sequentially snapping short pieces of white line, which was tied to the large anchor chain laid out on the buoy deck. The entire operation, from the release of the anchor: to the gyrating dance of the big can buoy as it slid off the buoy deck into the blue water was a symphony of motion. The Ivy did her part by maneuvering out from under the buoy once the anchor clump hit the bottom.

The Ivy now drifted away from the buoy, and the pinnacle of Cobb Seamount was now marked for the start of operations. Captain Boyce and the crew of the Ivy then set about deploying six buoys, each fitted with a tall staff and an orange pennant type flag to mark the periphery of the summit. With the buoy deployment completed, the Ivy was now on station at Cobb Seamount for the next eight days.

CHAPTER 24
TIME TO DIVE

The sea state was relatively calm with gentle rolling swells. It was still enough time left to make a couple of dives. Vince and I were the first divers. Our mission was to find some rock samples and a suitable location to deploy and activate the explosive anchor. We were hoping that the explosive anchor would be successful and would provide Ivy with a secure mooring on the undersea mountain. Previous attempts by other ships to moor on the mountain using a conventional anchor were unsuccessful due to the smooth hard rock bottom. The anchor would either slide across the bottom without catching, or become permanently stuck in some rock crevasse resulting in the loss of the anchor.

    Vince and I dressed into our diving gear and the Ivy dropped a temporary buoy in a potentially good spot in 130 feet of water. The rubber Zodiac boat was lowered over the side. Bob Lium, Vince, Chief Sheats and I got aboard. The chief would be our topside diving officer and Bob would drive the Zodiac boat. We ran the Zodiac boat over and tied up to the temporary marker buoy. There was sufficient anchor weight on the buoy line to hold the Zodiac and provide a stable descending line to the bottom.

    Vince and I put on twin tanks and weight belts and conducted our pre-dive safety checks. Before we started the dive, the chief wanted to take a depth reading using a short two and a half foot long fishing pole with a marked line to verify the depth. He verified the depth at 135 feet. At that depth for our planned dive time, we would be obligated to a short decompression stop 10 feet below the surface at the end of the dive.

After donning my fins and mask I was the first one to enter the water by rolling backwards off the side of the Zodiac. After plunging into the water, I immediately rolled over face down and grabbed the descending line attached to the mooring buoy. Now, I found myself staring down the descending line through shroud of bubbles created by my entry. As the bubbles dissipated I saw the descending line leading down into the blue void.

Suddenly, I saw them. About 15 feet below me swimming slowly around the descending line, were two large white tip sharks. I immediately pulled my head above water and yelled "SHARKS!! Two big white tips right below me!" the chief reacted by thrusting his small fishing pole into my hand to use to fend off the sharks in case they attacked! Boy! did that give me confidence! I could see the headlines, "**Large shark caught off Washington Coast. An arm with a diver's watch and a short fishing pole were found inside the animal.**"

As if I had totally lost my mind, I took the Chiefs' pole and dove for the largest of the two sharks. Miraculously, it turned away and streaked off into the blue void with its partner in trail. I bobbed back to the surface and announced that the sharks had gone, then I heard the splash as Vince entered the water. When he swam over next to me at the buoy I remarked "thanks for coming in to help me fight those sharks Vince." Vince took out his snorkel and gave me a big grin and retorted "my mama didn't raise no fools!"

With the sharks vanquished at least temporarily, we synchronized our time with each other and the Chief and started the dive. Once on the bottom we explored the immediate area and found that the rock bottom in this area was quite uneven and irregular and would not provide a good level place for the explosive anchor. After spending our bottom time on a circular search around the anchor, we started up the descending line stopping 10 feet below the Zodiac boat to take our mandatory decompression stop.

We had only been on the stop a few minutes when the two large white tips sharks returned. They didn't come as close this time and were content to mill around in the distance just barely visible. That was just fine with Vince and me, and we finished our decompression stop feeling a little uneasy with the large sharks close.

Safely back in the Zodiac boat and headed for the Ivy, the Chief recounted Vince's reaction when I entered the water and immediately announced the presence of large sharks. He said Vince was starting his backward roll into the water when I hollered "SHARKS". At that moment Vince was falling backward into the water with 80 pounds of tanks strapped to his back. The chief said Vince defied all the laws of physics when he stopped his backward momentum at over 45°and somehow managed to return to a sitting position on the side of the Zodiac. I guess the thought of being eaten by a large shark might create amazing powers of self-preservation!

When Vince and I got aboard the Ivy, we briefed the next dive team. We got their total attention we told them about the size of the sharks we saw. I suggested that on this dive they take along "Sharkbillys," short lengths of small diameter pipe about three feet long with a sharp point on one end and a bicycle handle grip on the other. The *"Sharkbilly"* had proven effective in fending off small to medium sized sharks when they get too close for comfort.

The next divers were excited to make a dive on the mountain, but a little disturbed by the shark sighting. The dive was in a new location and was uneventful. Sharks were sighted, but they kept well away from the diving station and the divers reported that the area looked promising for rock samples, and except for one small area, offered little in the way of the site location for the explosive anchor.

One more team dive verified the second team's findings. Operations were concluded for the day. We debriefed our divers and had a team meeting to plan and discuss the next day's operations. Regarding the shark sightings, I suggested that we request all shipboard garbage dumping be done after all the daily diving operations were concluded. Chief seats concurred and said he would pass that request to Captain Boyce.

On day two of the mission, dive teams searched for loose rock samples, instruments that were placed on the mountain by previous oceanographic expeditions, and a suitable site to place the explosive anchor. Several team dives were conducted that day and several types of sharks were sighted by the divers. Most of the larger sharks kept their distance, but some smaller blue sharks would come very close to the divers while they were on the decompression stop. The rest of the dives on day two were unable to locate a suitable location for the explosive anchor test, but Charles Berkland, now Dr. Berkland, a Marine Biologist from the University of Washington could make observations and collect samples for a study of the marine life of the Cobb Seamount

On day three of the mission, the second dive team of the day found a nice flat area to place the explosive anchor and marked the area with a buoy to the surface. None of the divers reported seeing any large sharks, but remarked about the small 5 to 6 foot blue sharks that came close enough to brush their legs while on the decompression stop. Two of the divers used the "*Sharkbillys*" to fend off a couple of sharks that got too close.

A third dive team re-examined the area found by the previous team and they sent up several small inflatable buoys marking the boundary of the level area, so the Ivy could lower the Explosive Anchor on to the most level spot. The area they marked was 130 feet deep, and the divers reported that the anchor launcher would probably rest on the bottom at about a seven-degree angle. The navy civil engineers determined that the angle would be acceptable.

CHAPTER 25
THE EXPLOSIVE ANCHOR

The rest of the morning was spent moving the huge explosive anchor with the ships crane to a position alongside the buoy deck where the anchor launcher was suspended over the water. Captain Boyce was adamant about not loading the propellant charge in the launcher until the anchor projectile was clear of the deck. He didn't want any possibility of a premature detonation that would sink the Ivy, or as we joked about headlines back home that might read **"*Explosive Anchor Pins Coast Guard Ship to Seamount!*"**

The explosive anchor was an impressive device! It was about 10 feet in diameter at the base which was a ring built like a huge heavy steel doughnut. There were three steel beams welded at 120° around the base they angled 12 feet up to a smaller steel ring about 4 feet in diameter, giving it the appearance of an Indian tepee with three large poles and minus the cover. The anchor projectile as it was called, was a huge steel three-bladed arrowhead with jagged edges. At the top of each blade was a steel bale to which we could attach our mooring line once the anchor was embedded in the rock. The blades were about four and a half feet long, three feet wide at the top tapering down to a sharp point. Welded to the top of the arrowhead anchor was a metal cylinder about 12 inches in diameter and about 3 feet long. This cylinder would be filled with an explosive and would serve to blast the steel arrowhead into the solid basalt rock, at least in theory that was the way it was supposed to work.

Engineering studies predicted that the projectile would penetrate the rock, holding fast to the serrated edges of the arrowhead blades. Divers could then fasten the Ivy's mooring line to the embedded anchor providing a secure mooring for our mission and other missions in the future

After the explosive anchor was loaded, Captain Boyce maneuvered the Ivy into position so the deck crew could lower the huge explosive anchor to the bottom next to the site marker buoys. Once the anchor was on the bottom, the team of divers was sent down the mooring line to check the position of the anchor. They returned to the surface requesting that the Ivy move the launcher about 10 feet east from its present position.

The divers then moved away from the anchor site and floated on the surface next to the Zodiac boat and safely away from the ship while the Ivy relocated the anchor. The divers now returned to the anchor line and made one more dive to do a quick survey. They returned to the surface and reported that the explosive anchor was in a suitable position for launching. Gene Smith, the Project engineer from the Naval Engineering Laboratory gave the final go ahead for the firing of the explosive anchor.

Now the diving team of John Goode and Bob Lium would dive down to the anchor location to remove the lowering line and install the detonating primer in the explosive anchor propellant.

John Goode was an engineer from Rocket Research Corporation. It was their propellant that was being used in the launcher. This was a potentially dangerous dive! If the explosive anchor were prematurely detonated with divers on the bottom near the launcher, the explosive concussion would kill both divers.

After arming the anchor, the divers attached wires from a large spool to the detonating primer. The divers then spooled out the detonating wire as they surfaced from the dive and the Zodiac crew hauled the large spool of wire into the Zodiac. The divers were recovered into the Zodiac boat and they radioed the Ivy that the explosive anchor was primed and ready to fire. Commander Boyce sailed the Ivy a safe distance from the pinnacle and the Zodiac crew moved the rubber boat about 200 yards from the pinnacle paying out the detonating wire.

With everyone clear of the explosive anchor area, John Goode detonated the primer. A distinct thud was felt through the hull of the Ivy and seconds later, a huge boil appeared on the surface of the water directly above the anchor site! The explosive anchor had fired and now it was time to see if the anchoring test was a success. Chief Sheats suggested if we wait about an hour before we sent another team of divers down to see if the shot had successfully embedded the anchor. I agreed that the short wait might be advisable in case the explosion had drawn in some large curious sharks!

Chief Sheats and Jim Washburn made the inspection dive and reported that the anchor projectile penetrated the basalt rock tipped at about twenty-degrees. The visible portion of the flukes showed considerable damage. There was a section broken off on one fluke and the barbs on the other flukes were bent. There was also a hairline fracture running through the portion of the anchor that was buried in the rock. The heavy steel anchor launcher was lying on its side about five feet from the anchor. The test was less successful than we had hoped. The portion of the anchor that was buried in the rock did offer a possibility of a mooring for the Ivy, but because the sea state was building and the wind direction was unfavorable, it was decided to wait until next day to attempt to moor the ship to the anchor, weather permitting.

The next morning, our first two dive teams were successful in getting the Ivy moored to the explosive anchor. The rest of the day was spent deploying various instruments on the pinnacle that would measure surge and other oceanographic factors. It was planned to recover the instruments on a mission the following year. The instruments were carefully located near known landmarks on the pinnacle and three Numec transmitting beacons were deployed in strategic spots to facilitate the location of the pinnacle and the instruments by divers on next year's mission.

The weather was getting ugly and all diving operations were suspended due to a rapidly building sea. Soon it was evident that we were in for our first storm 270 miles out into the Pacific Ocean.

WORKING ON THE EXPLOSIVE ANCHOR.

DIVERS IN THE ZODIAC HELPING TO SET UP FOR THE EXPLOSIVE ANCHOR LAUNCH.

DIVER SEARCHING FOR A PLACE TO SET THE EXPLOSIVE ANCHOR.

TYPICAL OCEAN CONDITIONS FOR DIVING ON THE COBB SEAMOUNT.

CHAPTER 26
THE COBB STORM

The Ivy was battened down in anticipation of some rough weather. Sometime in the early evening, the explosive anchor broke loose and the Ivy drifted off the pinnacle of the Cobb Seamount. The ship was forced to start engines and steam staying close to the mountaintop. The conditions worsened and the Ivy pitched and rolled in the building sea. The area near the pinnacle became too rough for safety and the Ivy steamed away from the pinnacle for smoother waters. Through the night the waves got higher and higher and no one slept very well as the Ivy pitched her bow into the waves.

In the morning, we were taking waves over the bow and Captain Boyce issued orders that no one was allowed outside on deck without a life jacket, and no one was allowed outside accept crew members with a duty assignment. The ride was getting miserable and anyone that was susceptible to seasickness was stricken! For those of us who were tolerant, it was a matter of hanging on!

The ocean around the seamount rebelled against us. For two days, every task aboard, was difficult due to the sometimes violent motions of the ship. Captain Boyce ordered that any of the crew assigned duties on the outer decks were to hook up to a life line to assure that no one was washed overboard. Getting washed overboard in those seas was surely a fatal event!

Even though most of the crew didn't seem to be too interested in eating, the cooks still did their best to provide us with meals. When you did get to the mess deck to eat, you had to wrap your arm around a stanchion pole next to the mess table and hold on to your plate while you tried to eat the food that was trying to slide off your plate on to the table. Eating in that storm was a wild experience and not very satisfying!

It was the afternoon of the second day of the storm and during the worst of the pitching and rolling, I happened to be able to see into the gallery as the cooks were struggling to make the dinner meal. Everything in the galley was swinging, rolling, or sliding. The poor cooks were at their wits end trying to get anything to hold still so they could cook it!

As I watched the galley staff struggling with their tasks, Captain Boyce entered the companionway and stopped for a moment at a spot where he could see the crew working in the galley. Suddenly the ship lurched and rolled with a large wave! A huge pot of hot mashed potatoes started sliding along the stainless-steel table that ran lengthwise of the galley. All the cooks were thrown off balance and no one could get to the sliding pot before it slammed against the bulkhead and bounced over the retaining lip of the preparation table. The huge pot of hot mashed potatoes was now airborne in the middle of the galley!

The closest to the flying pot was the chief cook, a First-Class Petty Officer by the name of Rafferty. As Rafferty regained his balance and realized that he could not save the mashed potatoes, he uttered a profanity at the flying pot, and in desperation, drop kicked it across the galley! Hot mashed potatoes went everywhere, and the pandemonium stopped with the entire galley crew cursing and wiping mashed potatoes off their bodies.

Now, all this chaos was observed by the captain and I expected some sort of a reaction! Instead, Captain Boyce just shook his head and walked off down the companionway. Later, I mentioned to Captain Boyce that I too, had witnessed the mashed potato disaster. He smiled at me and said "Spence, you're probably wondering why I didn't get upset by the incident. Any captain worth his salt knows better than to mess with his cooks in a storm".

CHAPTER 27

BACK TO WORK

The next day the storm settled down although the sea was very rough with big swells. The Ivy sailed back to the pinnacle, and there we encountered huge swells about 30 feet from crest to trough and about 400 feet from peak to peak! An unusual condition caused by the seamount pinnacle. Later in the day, Roland white and I made a dive on the pinnacle to observe conditions on the bottom during the huge swells. With the ship rolling in the gigantic swells, Roland and I had to jump from the buoy deck and swim away from the ship rapidly to avoid being sucked under the ship as her bow came out of the water on the swells! As the ship rose and fell on the crests and the troughs, the buoy deck where Roland and I waited to make our entry into the water, was sometimes even with the surface and sometimes 30 feet above it! We had to time our jump so that we didn't have far to drop into the water.

Once Roland and I were in the water, and started swimming away from the ship toward the buoy and descending line, we looked back toward the ship and much to our surprise, we could see the ship's propeller through the wave at it road up on a swell. The swells were monstrous. At times, Roland and I felt that we were 40 to 50 feet below the bottom of the ship when we were in a trough. It was rather uncomfortable being in the water that close to the ship in these conditions.

When we reached the buoy, I signaled Rolland to set our bottom timers and start the dive. Once we left the surface and descended below 40 or 50 feet, the surface movement diminished. The depth to the bottom was 140 feet. As we came within 20 or 30 feet of the bottom, we found ourselves surging back and forth over the bottom. We would be swept about 30 feet one way, hover still for a moment, then be swished back in the opposite direction about 30 feet. It was impossible to resist the surging motion of the water!

The descending line from the surface buoy was tending to the south with a strong north wind blowing on the surface. What was strange, was that the surge on the bottom at 130 feet was east and west, 90 degrees to the direction of the descending line. Apparently, this was an anomaly created by the pinnacle of the mountain and the movement of the ocean in the rough sea.

What was interesting, was watching a huge school of large rockfish swished back and forth with us in the surge. They hung motionless and did not try to swim when the surge was moving them. When this surge stopped for a moment at the end of the cycle, the fish would quickly swim in the direction they wanted to go. After watching them for a few moments, Roland and I took a lesson from the fish and only swam when the surge stopped for a moment. It worked OK, but it felt strange to be totally at the mercy of the surge most of the time.

With that strong surging motion, we couldn't accomplish much except to observe conditions on the bottom. Neither Roland nor I wanted to get too far from the descending line! Soon, our bottom time was up, we ascended to 10 feet below the surface for a short decompression stop. We saw no sharks on this dive. Apparently, the surface conditions were too rough for any shark activity. Roland and I waited for the Ivy to work her way close enough to us so that we could swim from the buoy to a position alongside the buoy deck.

The deck crew had rigged the boom and the chain diving stage over the side for us. The stage was lowered into the water so Roland and I could get aboard and be hauled up onto the buoy deck. The problem was that the Ivy was pitching in the huge swells and rolling about 20° from side to side. The chain stage was being dunked 15 to 20 feet underwater and then pulled nearly out of the water during the surges. Roland and I had to stay clear of the stage and try to time our boarding so we didn't get hit and injured. Boarding the stage in that sea state was a big challenge.

Finally, safe aboard the Ivy, I advised Chief Sheats not to allow any other divers off the ship in these conditions. The chief concurred. When we were debriefed on our dive, we recounted the experience we had in the strong surge. When we reported that the surge propelled us about 30 feet each way and 90 degrees to the direction of the descending line, they were surprised! One would think from direction of the movement of the surface water, the surge would be in the direction of the swells. This information was significant to understanding the underwater conditions over the pinnacle of a shallow seamount, and a first-hand observation of actual conditions during heavy seas.

In the last two days on the seamount, we deployed the Nereus surge meter and a small wave meter. Vince and I drew the task of setting up the wave meter on the seamount. A company engineer in charge of the wave meter was with us on the ship and he briefed us on exactly how he wanted us to set up and secure the instrument. First, it had to be oriented to magnetic north and secured to the mountain. This would be accomplished by using a concrete anchoring gun called a *"ramset"* to pin the four leg pads of the instrument to the hard basalt rock bottom.

The instrument was housed in a watertight metal cylinder about 18 inches in diameter. There were two Brass rods about one quarter inch in diameter projecting out of the top of the device. The rods were bent at an angle and projected in opposite directions. At the tip of each rod, was a bright fluorescent orange Styrofoam ball about 7 inches in diameter. The engineer was adamant about us not damaging the balls during the dive. We assured him that we would be very careful with the instrument.

The instrument weighed about 60 pounds out of the water but would only weigh about 33 pounds in the water due to the buoyancy of the housing. We loaded the instrument into the Zodiac boat and Vince and I boarded the Zodiac with the topside diving crew of Jim Washburn and Roland white. We moored the Zodiac to the large can buoy that we had deployed earlier and Vince and I entered the water. The topside crew lowered the instrument and we guided it carefully down alongside the can buoy anchor chain. When we reach the bottom, we disconnected the lowering line and signaled for the topside crew to retrieve the line.

Vince and I then moved the instrument away from the nine-ton concrete clump anchoring the can buoy and found a relatively flat spot where we could set up and anchor the instrument. Our depth was 140 feet, and as usual we were surrounded by a large school of huge red snapper and rockfish. On previous dives, the big fish were somewhat of a bother. They were obnoxious and not afraid to swim right up to the divers and try to eat anything that might be dangling, or was small enough to fit in their mouths. They even chomped down on one diver's depth gauge, trying to pull it off his wrist!

Vince and I carefully positioned the instrument on the flat spot and used our specially designed underwater compass to orient the instrument to magnetic north. Then we pinned the foot pads of the unit to the rock surface with the ramset tool. The explosive shots from ramset gun attracted a large crowd of rockfish and snapper and one huge fish which we couldn't identify. Vince and I checked the placement and integrity of the instrument. We noticed that the two fluorescent orange Styrofoam balls were compressed due to the depth and were now about three inches in diameter. We assumed that this was to be expected by the engineers.

With the instrument, securely in place, we picked up our tools and backed away from it a few yards. That was all the opening needed for the two huge snappers that immediately attacked the Styrofoam balls and ate them! Vince and I had to clamp our regulators to our mouths while we were laughing to keep from drowning! So much, for terrestrial engineering, and survival of equipment placed on the ocean bottom!!

With the mission accomplished (sort of) we ascended the can buoy mooring chain to 20 feet below the surface, where we moved to the decompression station below the Zodiac boat. After our decompression, we boarded the Zodiac boat and returned to the Ivy. We had no sooner stepped aboard the Ivy, when our wave meter engineer appeared for a briefing. He immediately started asking questions about his instrument.

I knew I could never keep a straight face, so I let Vince to all the talking! "Did you find a nice flat spot?" he asked. "We did." Vince replied. "Are you sure that you aligned the instrument arrow with magnetic north?" "It was a perfect alignment." Vince answered. "Were you able to fasten the instrument to the bottom securely?" "Yes, all three pads were securely fastened with three ramset charges per pad."

With each positive confirmation from Vince, I could see that the engineer was starting to relax, showing a relieved and satisfied smile. Looking very pleased, the engineer started to walk away when Vince called out after him. "By the way, those orange Styrofoam balls, where they very important?" Vince asked with a perfectly straight face. "Why, you didn't damage them did you?" the engineer asked, his face showing great concern. "Oh no, we were very careful with the unit and after we finished securing the instrument to the bottom, they were just fine." Vince reassured. Then, after a short pause, he added. "They were just fine until two big fish ate them!" The engineers face dropped a foot and I had to turn away and muffle my mouth. The poor engineer shuffled off totally dejected, and to make matters worse, there was loud laughter that arose from all the Coast Guard and diving crew that was within earshot of the briefing. I guess in the future, that company will have to make their equipment "snapper proof!"

With all the instruments deployed and the last dive team aboard, Captain Boyce gave order to set sail for Astoria. Ivy left the seamount around 6:00 PM and we arrived at Port Astoria at around 2:00 PM the next day.

I AM FASTENING THE SURGE METER TO THE SEAMOUNT WITH THE RAMSET GUN

CHAPTER 28
STORIES FROM COBB

There were far too many good stories during the preparations for and the excursions of those eight missions to the Cobb Seamount, and though I would like to tell them all to you, I fear this book would be far too lengthy, but since I cannot resist, I will tell you the ones most vivid in my mind.

There was a total of eight diving missions to the Cobb Seamount from 1968 through 1975. One aboard the ESSA ship Oceanographer, one aboard the Naval Research Ship Bartlett, another aboard the U.S. Army Coastal Freighter FS 313 and the rest aboard the Coast Guard Cutters Ivy, Cactus, and Iris.

The missions were real adventures, and I must say that if I had to go to sea for a tough diving mission, I would want to go with a crew of a Coast Guard Buoy tender captained by Commander Random Boyce. It was the Sea Use III-A mission that we had some real excitement! Again, we sailed out of Astoria with the Coast Guard. Captain Boyce was our skipper, but the Ivy had been de-commissioned and this time we sailed aboard the Cactus.

It was Chief Mac's last year before retirement and this time when we arrived at the dock, he was happy to see us. Although he and Vince got off to a rough start, the chief observed Vince to be a natural seaman. When the chief found out that Vince was interested in rigging and heavy ships tackle, he took Vince under his wing and taught him a lot about working on the deck. Vince ate it up! He learned so fast and became so proficient, that Captain Boyce and Chief Mac allowed him to serve with the crew on special sea and anchor detail. When the chief found out that Vince knew how to weld and splice wire rope, he spent hours with Vince on his off-duty time teaching Vince everything he wanted to learn. By the end of Sea Use II, they had become good friends.

As we stood on the dock next to the ship, Chief Mac came out to the buoy deck. He saw Vince and waived for him to come aboard. As Vince walked to the gangway to board the ship, the chief disappeared into the interior of the ship. When Vince reached the buoy deck, the chief reappeared with a package in his hand. He greeted Vince with a handshake and gave him the package. In the package was a blue coast guard work shirt with a Third-Class Petty Officer's rank. He told Vince that the officers and crew who knew him had voted to make him an honorary Third-Class for the mission.

Vince was elated and immediately when into the forward locker to change. In a minute, he returned wearing the shirt. With his blue dungarees and work boots, you couldn't tell him from one of the official coast guard crew. I believe that the only time Vince ever took off that shirt during the mission was to get into his diving gear.

I was serving a double role on this mission. Chief Sheats had recommended me as a diving supervisor and the Sea Use Program which was designated as an oceanographic expedition, needed someone aboard to act as Chief Scientist. On this mission, I could fill both roles.

The trip out to the seamount was smooth and the sea state at the mountain was calm with long gentle swells. Not very often, does the ocean above Cobb Seamount offer such great diving conditions. As we arrived at the undersea mountain, Captain Boyce and I decided to run some operation bends drills before beginning diving operations.

We loaded one of the two rubber Zodiac boats over the side and sent one of our new team divers to check the outboard motor and warm it up for the training exercises. Our young diver dressed in his diving wet suit, climbed down the Jacob's ladder, a ladder made of hemp line and wooden steps and boarded the Zodiac. In his excitement to be at the seamount, and doing something as a member of the team, his youthful enthusiasm began to cause a disease that plagues everyone at times. We in the diving field call it **"HYCUMFLUKIE"**. It manifests with no warning, causing a sudden surge of fecal matter to the brain, rendering the victim incompetent for several minutes!

Stricken with the disease, our rookie diver, released the Zodiac boat from the Cactus without waiting for the other experienced Sea Use diver that we had assigned to help him. He then became focused on starting the outboard motor. After several pulls on the starter rope, it roared to life and belted a plume of smoke that drifted away in the wind.

With the motor running, he engaged the propeller and started sailing away from the Cactus at about a 45° angle from the rear of the ship. As he sailed out into the calm blue water, he was totally engrossed in manipulating the throttle and adjusting the choke for the best smoothness of the motor. As he fiddled with his adjustments, the Zodiac picked up speed and was starting a large left circle. It completed the circle about 30 yards from the Cactus and headed straight for the side of the ship.

All the ship's crew who were watching including the captain, executive officer, and most of the Sea Use diving team stared in disbelief as the Zodiac doing about 15 knots impacted the side of the 180-foot ship directly below the bridge wing! The front of the Zodiac folded up like an accordion against the steel side of the ship, and paused just long enough for our diver to be thrown from the back of the Zodiac to the bow and almost off the boat while the tough little rubber boat rebounded off the side of the ship!

Our rookie diver was now scrambling back to shut off the motor as nearly the entire ships company howled with laughter. When the laughter faded and the Zodiac was drifting silently along the side of the ship directly below the bridge. Captain Boyce leaned over the bridge wing and shouted down to our poor embarrassed diver. **"what's the matter? Couldn't you see us?"** The crew went into hysterics! It was mortifying enough to our new, inexperienced diver to have hit the ship, but the quick-thinking coast guard crew wasn't done with him just yet. As he climbed up the "*Jacob's* *ladder*" and stepped onto the deck, a First-Class Petty Officer handed him a Coast Guard moving violation citation.

When Captain Boyce saw, the ticket being handed to our diver, he used the ship's loudspeaker and summoned him up to the bridge. When our beleaguered young diver appeared in the wheelhouse, Captain Boyce said with a straight face "(name) you'll have to fill out some paperwork." Then he added in a serious tone, "You know. ramming the United States Coast guard cutter is a Federal offense. Our poor diver was on the verge of tears when everyone including Captain Boyce broke down and started laughing. "Relax son" He said. "We were just having a little fun at your expense. The ticket was just a joke. You're not in any trouble. Just keep your eyes toward the pointy end of the boat from now on!" "yes, sir." replied our diver, a total look of relief on his face. After our diver left the bridge, everyone had another good laugh. Unfortunately, no unprecedented act committed aboard ship is without reminders from the crew. For the rest of the mission, our young diver was nicknamed **"*Captain Zodiac.*"**

CLIMBING THE JACOB'S LADDER IN FULL DIVING GEAR

CHAPTER 29
THE SEARCH

The main objective of the Sea Use III-A mission was to locate and recover all the instruments we had deployed on Sea Use II. Much to the Numec company's disappointment, none of the three underwater locator beacons were working; which meant that the other instruments would be more difficult to find and would require some extensive diver searches.

A major complication for our ability to search a lot of the area on a single dive was the obligation to decompression. At the depth, we would be searching, we would only have about 30 minutes per team before the decompression requirements exceeded our Sea Use operations limits. To have adequate bottom time at depths which range from 140 two 160 feet we had mandatory decompression stops before we could return to the surface. This meant that the divers would have to stay near the anchor line leading up to the Zodiac boat and the decompression station.

The decompression station system consisted of a line 30 feet long with a lead ball weighing 30 pounds at one end. The other end was secured to the Zodiac boat. The line was marked with a 20 foot stop marker and a 10 foot stop marker and at the 30 foot stop depth there were two hoses each fitted with the breathing end of a scuba regulator. The regulator hoses were connected to a large compressed air tank in the Zodiac. If each either diver was low on air after returning from the dive, they would both have adequate air from the surface to last them through the required underwater decompression.

The moment the divers were safely on the first decompression stop, the Zodiac would untie from its anchor buoy and drift free with the divers decompressing below the drifting boat. When the decompression was complete, the divers would be helped onto the pontoon sides of the Zodiac. Both divers would lie on their stomach on each side of the Zodiac still dressed in full gear. The Zodiac crew would then take the divers over to the Cactus. The crew of the Cactus would lower the chain stage into the water to pick up the divers and lift them up onto the buoy deck where dive team members could help them out of their gear.

This staging aboard technique was very efficient and quick. However, it could get very exciting if the sea was rough and your timing was off. Sometimes there could be a slight delay in starting the lift after the diver boarded the stage. If the sea was too rough, the diver would be plunged up and down through the surface several times, trying to hang on and keep from losing their masks and other pieces of equipment. To keep from injuring or embarrassing oneself, there was a definite knack to riding the stage in rough water.

To get the divers off the ship without having to load all the diving gear into the Zodiac boat and have the divers dress into their gear in the small rubber boat at the dive site, the Cactus would maneuver to a close position downwind from a small buoy marking the area for starting the dive. The divers would be dressed into full diving gear, ready to jump from the buoy deck into the water.

Normally the jump would be about 10 feet from the buoy deck to the water in calm seas. In heavy seas and the ship was rolling, you could almost step off the buoy deck when the deck rolled toward the water and when the ship rolled away from the water, it could be one heck of a drop.

The consequences of the long drop besides the ocean trying to tear off all your gear was the fact that you were very close to the side of the ship and when you hit the water, the ship could roll back and suck you under the hull! You would have several tons of steel hull crashing down on your soft little rubber coated body! Most of our diving team was very good at avoiding the experience.

Once the ship was in position near the dive site, a handheld aluminum reel called a "*Saf-line reel*" containing about 200 feet of small gauge nylon line was thrown out into the water a few yards from the ship. The reel would sink to the bottom and about 140 feet of line with two inflatable buoys on the end would create a visual descending line to the top of the seamount.

The divers then jumped from the buoy deck and swam over to the yellow popper buoys. The Cactus, her propellers stopped for safety would drift away from the dive site, and the Zodiac boat with our topside tending crew would join the divers at the descending line. After safety checks were made and time was synchronized, the divers would begin their dive.

Once the divers were on the bottom, they would pick up the aluminum Saf-line reel and start a "free ranging" search using an underwater compass. As the divers swam along the bottom 140 feet down, the two little yellow buoys would be towed along at the surface. The Zodiac boat with the tending crew, our topside safety diver and our decompression station would say alongside the yellow buoys and follow the divers across the pinnacle while they searched for the lost instruments. The Zodiac with the decompression station and topside crew would always be directly above the divers. The "SCUBA open ocean free ranging system was developed and perfected by the Sea Use diving team. It allowed us to cover large areas of the pinnacle despite our short limited 30-minute bottom time.

      Captain Butch, as he allowed me to call him, and I had a friendly rivalry. I knew that the ship's officers hated to be delayed on any operation by their own crew, let alone some group of civilians using their ship as a diving platform. I told the dive team that I wanted them to ready everything for the day's diving the night before, even if it took all night to do it, somewhat an exaggeration. I said I wanted a team mandate that the ship would never wait on the divers to start work, and that we would always be waiting on the ship. I think that the word of our mandate somehow got back to Captain Butch and he similarly rallied his crew and the competition was on!

      At first, I think the dive team saw our mandate as extra work and sort of an inconvenience, but after a few days, they got into the spirit of the thing and I had their full support. On our first diving day, my number one diving team was dressed into full gear and sitting on the buoy deck diving station ready bench at 7:00 AM. The entire diving crew manned their stations and even the diving doctor was standing by with his chamber operators. The ship's crew wasn't quite ready for diving operations this early, and when they found out we were waiting, they scrambled to get the ship ready to support the dive. I glanced up to the bridge and I could see Captain Butch shouting orders to get the ship in gear. I put on a big smile and pointed at Captain Butch, Diving crew one, Ship zero.

The day was a busy one with the diving crew and the ship hurrying to accomplish as many tasks as we could while the weather and the sea were co-operating. We accomplished a lot that day and the diving team was pretty beat from the combination of repetitive deep dives, decompression and tending duties aboard the small Zodiac boat in somewhat rough, but workable conditions.

During one of the dives one of the team divers was accidently pulled up to the surface from the 20-foot decompression stop. When our safety diver free dove down to take an underwater camera from the divers. A strap from the camera got hooked around the tank valve of one of the divers and as the safety diver swam back to the surface he accidently pulled the diver up 15 feet before he realized the problem. Immediately the Zodiac crew went into the "*Missed D*" procedure and notified the ship to move a little closer to the Zodiac in the event of a "*Bends*" occurrence. Fortunately, the Missed decompression procedure was successful and the dive ended uneventfully.

We made eight team dives that day and I dove in rotation with my team. When the final team got back aboard the ship around

6:30 PM everyone including the deck crew and the ships officers were tired. The evening meal was later than usual and afterwards the diving crew set about preparing for tomorrows dives.

It was probably the long day and the fatigue that caused us to overlook checking to see if we had enough filled air tanks for the next days' dives. Even though the divers and the ship's crew were both ready at 7:00 AM for the start of work, we had to delay the fourth team of divers while we filled some tanks. This caused the ship to wait about thirty minutes before we could resume diving. From the bridge Captain Butch smiled and pointed his finger at me!

SEA USE DIVER READY TO TAKE A 12 FOOT JUMP OFF THE BUOY DECK INTO THE WATER

DIVING TEAM SWIMMING TOWARD THE POPPER BUOYS AND THEIR DESCENDING LINE TO THE TOP OF COBB SEAMOUNT

DIVER ON THE BOTTOM WITH THE SAF-LINE SEARCH REEL READY TO START HIS MISSION

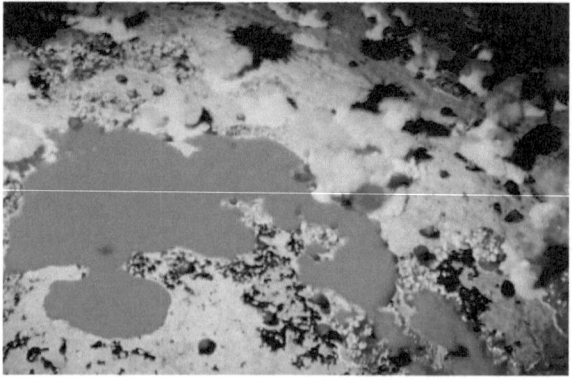

THE TOP OF THE SEAMOUNT IS COVERED IN CREAM-COLORED CORALINE ALGAE WITH PATCHES OF RED ENCRUSTING SPONGE. AND A LOT OF OTHER SEA LIFE

CHAPTER 30
THE GRANDCHILD EXPERIENCE

It was on my second dive of the Sea Use III-A mission that I had a "grandchild experience! That is an experience you call tell your grandchildren one day when you want to hold their attention. It was the first dive of the day. Kirby Johnson and I were the divers.

The morning was beautiful with perfect calm conditions for the dive. The ocean above Cobb Seamount was taking a break from her usual 8 to 15 foot swells and white caps. The water was deep blue and crystal clear, and both Kirby and I were quietly excited about the dive, as we dressed into our diving gear and performed the "buddy checks" on each other's equipment.

This was to be a quick dive to 130 feet, and if we could get a mooring line attached to one of the "Totem" anchors quickly, we would be able to ascend back to the surface with only a precautionary safety stop at 10 feet, and avoid the mandatory decompression stops required on longer dives.

Kirby and I were ready to go about the same time Captain Boyce maneuvered the Cactus into position downwind of the Zodiac boat. The Zodiac crew was holding station on a small orange buoy that had been anchored to one of the "Totem" anchors by the last search team. The temporary buoy line would guide us down to the pinnacle and the anchor.

When the ship was in position, the bridge gave the signal to stop the ships propellers, so there would be no chance of us drifting back under the ship toward huge turning propeller. When the ship stated to drift away from the drop area, Kirby and I were given the signal to jump from the buoy deck. It was about a 10 to 12 foot drop from the buoy deck to the water.

Suddenly, we were both in midair and made quite a splash, hitting the water in full gear with twin tanks. For a moment after submerging from the plunge, you could not see anything but froth and bubbles. It was always a scary feeling to have those bubbles dissipate, and find yourself staring at a 10 to 12-foot white tip shark just a few feet away! This was the moment in our operation when all the divers felt vulnerable. We were always wary of seeing large sharks when the bubbles cleared away. This time there was nothing but the limitless azure blue void and my diving buddy next to me.

Kirby and I used our fins and snorkels to cover the few yards to the Zodiac boat. We completed our final checks with the Zodiac crew. John Eriksen, one of our diving officers was our safety diver. He was in full wet suit with fins, mask and snorkel and enough weight on his belt to allow him to free dive to the decompression stops, the deepest at 30 feet. John was in the water next to the Zodiac boat where he could watch us as we swam down next to the line descending to the bottom. He would remain in the water during the entire dive, and keep a vigil for us to return to the decompression stops at the planned time. Since we had recent encounters with some large white tip sharks, and on occasion smaller oceanic blue sharks would make a run-on diver's dangling legs, John carried a sharkbilly. Our final checks complete, Kirby and I placed our regulators in our mouths and started down the descending line to the pinnacle of the mountain 130 feet below. As we descended we kept a watch on each other to make sure neither one of us stopped during the descent and we remained close until we reached the bottom.

Some divers may have to stop a moment to clear their ears. For Kirby and me, ear clearing was not a problem and we descended at a fast pace. I loved diving with my team. They were excellent divers. Suddenly, the top of the mountain was visible and the water was so clear for a moment you felt like you were flying and for some it might have provoked a "*fear of falling*" sensation.

As usual, the bottom was a spectacular sight with sparse patches of long filament algae, flowing a foot or so above the basalt rock bottom that was covered with a veneer of cream colored coralline algae. The ever-present schools of large red snapper and rock fish greeted us on our arrival at the "Totem" anchor.

As we reached bottom, one large snapper promptly swam to Kirby and tried to eat the shiny handle of the diving knife strapped to his leg. Kirby backed away a few feet, but that fish was determined to eat the knife. For a few moments, Kirby and the fish danced around the totem anchor with the fish making repeated attacks on the knife handle and Kirby kicking it away each time it got close to his leg.

The subliminal effects of Nitrogen Narcosis seemed to enhance the effect of any funny circumstance and made it easy to over react in a fit of laughter. I was almost amused into drowning while trying to breathe and laugh at the same time! The problem with laughing through your regulator underwater is that it is very difficult to maintain a good seal around your mouthpiece. If just a little bit of salt water was inhaled, the diver would be in big trouble!

Suddenly the underwater comedy show was interrupted when I saw Kirby take a swipe at the fish with the big metal shackle he held in his hand. The shackle! Oh, Oh! I glanced at my bottom timer. We had wasted about three minutes of our precious ten minute no decompression bottom time cavorting with this stupid fish! I signaled Kirby to bring the shackle to me at the totem anchor.

Meanwhile at the surface, the Zodiac had run a short distance to the Cactus which was holding station about 40 yards from the dive site. A large nylon mooring line with a large shackle on the end was lowered into the Zodiac from the buoy deck. The Zodiac then towed the line and shackle over to the diving station. After tying up to the station buoy, the Zodiac crew gave a sharp tug on the descending line that I could feel at the anchor. I immediately returned the signal by jerking the line.

On the surface, the crew fastened the heavy shackle around the descending line and began lowering it from the Zodiac while the large mooring line was fed out to the Zodiac by the deck crew on the Cactus. Kirby and I backed away from the large anchor and in a few seconds the huge shackle clanked against the anchor where the descending line was tied. We quickly moved in to remove the shackle from the descending line and attach it to one of the metal bales on the totem anchor.

With the shackle secured to the anchor, I signaled the Zodiac crew that the attachment had been made so they could release the mooring line and let the Cactus have it. Task accomplished! The Cactus was now moored to the totem anchor at Cobb Seamount.

I glanced at my bottom timer. We had one minute left and I signaled Kirby that we should start to the surface. Slowly, we ascended the line watching the bottom fade from sight as we reached the 30-foot decompression stop. At this depth, we would pause for a moment and check with our safety diver on the surface. He would give us an OK signal to let us know that our dive time was correct and we could ascend to the surface as planned. No decompression stop was required on this dive, but Kirby and I would take a precautionary stop at 10 feet for two minutes just to be on the safe side.

The hang off decompression stops were relatively boring with nothing to do but maintain depth and stare off into the blue void. Sometimes there was an array of large plankton suspended in the water at the surface and the strange looking planktonic critters were interesting to watch. Then, there were the sharks!

We were about a minute into our decompression stop when John free dove down in front of me and pointed out into the void with his sharkbilly. He pumped his arm and sharkbilly in one direction several times and then gave me the V hand sign for shark. He appeared excited and punctuated his sign by spanning his hands wide apart to indicate a large shark before swimming back to the surface. John had seen large sharks before on his dives and he was always Mr. Cool. I had never seen him show much emotion about the sharks.

I stared in the direction John had pointed and saw nothing. I assumed John had seen one of the larger white tips. As I continued staring into the void, a dark form gradually appeared in the distance and got larger and larger as it moved toward the decompression station. I glanced up to the surface at John who was now frantically pumping the sharkbilly in the direction of the approaching form.

As I stared at the dark form gliding our way, I realized that this was no white tip. Oh, my God! Its huge frontal area was mostly mouth. I could see rows of large white jagged teeth as it swam toward us with its mouth partly open. A small striped pilot fish was leading the way and I could see two remora parasite fish attached to the underbelly of this huge beast.

Now, there was no mistaking what was almost upon us. Only about 20 yards and closing fast was a very large Great White Shark, one of the monsters of the sea! This was a reputed man eater, and we were dangling on a line like bait! I couldn't tell exactly how large it was, but from estimates by my divers that were very close, we estimated it around 17 to 19 feet in length. That was big enough to eat divers!

As the huge fish closed in on us, I realized that Kirby was facing in the opposite direction and hadn't seen the great white yet, and I didn't want him to be eaten before he had a chance to see what was going to eat him, so I gave him a sharp nudge in the back and he turned in immediate response to my nudge. He was pressed against me at the decompression stop when he first sighted the great white. The huge shark was within 12 feet of us. Now, when you are 10 feet underwater and totally exposed to the main marine killing machine, you know what fear tastes like!

When Kirby saw the shark, he gave a groan and his body went ridged like it had turned to concrete. The huge fish glided past us showing incredible propulsion with no apparent motion, and then headed down into deeper water and faded from sight.

For a moment, Kirby and I were paralyzed with awe, staring after the disappearing shark. Then, as if a loud alarm bell had sounded, I awoke from my stupor and realized that if we were in the water and that big shark was near, Kirby, John and I were still monster bait. Quickly, I whirled around and gave Kirby the underwater "**let's get the hell out of here sign**." There wasn't such a sign, but whatever sign it was that I gave Kirby, He knew exactly what it meant!

In less than a second, and with decompression the farthest thing from our minds, we were on the surface alongside the Zodiac boat. We could hear the topside crew's loud exclamations, punctuated by expletives. "He was way bigger than the damn Zodiac!" someone shouted. "That dorsal fin looked like a small grey sailboat!" someone added. "Get those divers into the Zodiac!" shouted Roland White, our diving station officer. Now, that was a suggestion we were anxious to comply with!

Kirby and I were starting to remove our heavy gear so we could get into the boat, when John, our safety diver who had his head submerged keeping watch, suddenly lifted his head out of the water, spit out his snorkel and shouted "It's coming back!!" There was no time to get our gear off and get into the boat before it could get to us. I shouted for Roland to give Kirby and me the two small 38 cubic foot tanks with regulators that we sometimes used in emergencies. In a flash the crew grabbed the tanks, turned on the tank valves and pushed them over the side to us.

I quickly told Kirby to put in his regulator, stay close to me and if the shark came at us, we would push the free flow button on the small tank regulators and point them at the shark with the idea that a large stream of bubbles may turn it away. Kirby nodded and put in his regulator. In a moment, we were both underwater scanning for the big shark;

For a moment, we didn't see it, then, John pointed down into the depths. The sight that greeted us made me numb for a second! The great white was at a depth of about 50 feet. It was coming up right at us. Then to our amazement, John started a free dive directly at the shark with his sharkbilly extended ahead of him!

This was absolutely going to qualify as a grandchild experience! I quickly looked at Kirby who couldn't believe what he was seeing! I held the small tank regulator out in front of me and started swimming down right behind John, hoping that Kirby knew what I was going to do. He did, and he was right beside me, with the small tank regulator outstretched in front of him.

I would estimate the distance between John and the eating end of the monster was about 20 feet when Kirby and I simultaneously hit the purge buttons. Immediately, two 3 foot streams of compressed air shot out in front of us and filled the blue water with a wall of bubbles. The problem was that neither, Kirby; or I could see a thing, and we couldn't tell what was happening with the shark! In somewhat of a panic, I let off on the air, hoping that my first sight wouldn't be John's legs and fins sticking out of the shark's huge mouth!

Kirby must have had the same inclination, because, he had also let off on his purge button. As the curtain of bubbles cleared, I was relieved to see John, intact, headed back toward the surface from a depth of about 30 feet. I could also see the great white shark gliding back down into the depths. Apparently, between the sight of John and his sharkbilly and the great wall of bubbles, we had turned it around.

It then occurred to me that if the big shark was now swimming away from us that we should be swimming away from it! I gave Kirby another LGTHOOH sign and we immediately started to the surface and the safety of the Zodiac. Our normal egress routine was to remove our weight belts and hand them to our crew in the boat, then we would remove the heavy twin tanks and the crew would take them into the boat for us. As we neared the surface under the Zodiac, I motioned for Kirby to go up on one side as I headed for the other.

When we surfaced alongside the boat, we handed the small tanks to the boat crew. John was already in the boat, so we had no idea if that great white was going to make another try at us. I shouted to Kirby on the other side of the Zodiac and said that we had no time to do our normal egress. I told Kirby to just swim hard up on to the pontoon and have the boat crew haul him in, tanks and all. The topside crew responded immediately. I kicked as hard as I could with my fins and the boat crew pulled me up on to the starboard pontoon as Kirby was hauled up on the port side.

Roland was already releasing the Zodiac from the anchor buoy and within seconds the outboard motor was propelling us toward the Cactus. I don't know what the rest of the team was thinking at that time, although there was some residual excitement. Me, I was offering up a silent prayer to my guardian angel!

Half way to the ship, we could see the great white shark's dorsal fin on the surface about 50 yards from us. From our low vantage in the Zodiac it did look like a small grey sail boat! As we approached the ship we could see three Coast Guardsmen up on the flying bridge with rifles. We knew that rifles were useless against this big shark, but we appreciated the gesture.

We abandoned the usual procedure of rolling off the Zodiac into the water and riding the stage aboard. Everyone was perfectly happy with climbing from the small boat up the Jacobs ladder to the buoy deck! When everyone was safely aboard the Cactus, we watched the huge fin circling the orange buoy where we were diving.

It was probably wondering where its dinner went! Since **JAWS** was with us now, we contemplated what to do about our new problem.

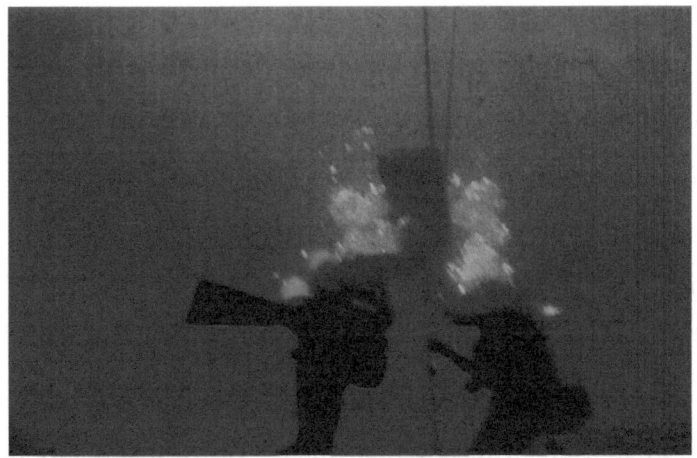

DIVERS ON DECOMPRESSION STOPS ARE VUNERABLE TO A SHARK ATTACK

A GREAT WHITE SHARK 16 TO 17 FEET IN LENGTH WITH VERY LARGE TEETH!

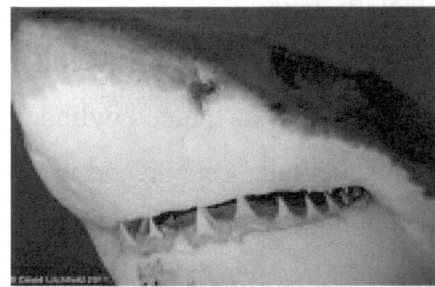

TEETH LIKE THESE!!

CHAPTER 31
JAWS RETURNS

The new problem was that jaws was in the area and we virtually had no protection when we were in the water. It was either stop diving and go home, keep diving and hope that the big shark would go away; or at least stay curious about our divers and not try to eat any.

We polled the team and they opted to continue operations. Captain Boyce gave orders that no garbage was to be dumped overboard until late at night when Cactus was off the pinnacle and a few miles away from the diving area. The next day we started diving operations at 0800. There was no sign of the great white. We ran five teams of divers that day and there were no sightings of the large shark.

One team located three of the six instruments we had placed on the mountain the year before. Unfortunately, all of them were heavily damaged. At that time, we didn't know whether the winter ocean conditions had caused the damage, or that Russian and Japanese trawlers which were known to fish the mountain had dislodged and dragged the instruments with their nets.

On the next diving day, we recovered two more instruments one of which was the Nereus surge meter. This was a metal cylinder about one foot in diameter and about four feet tall. On one end were three metal legs with pads for the instrument to stand on. On the top of the unit was a wire mesh cage surrounding the mechanical motion sensors for detecting the surge and current conditions on the top of the seamount.

Although the unit was found slightly bent up and lying on its side, we were hopeful that it had remained in its anchored position on the pinnacle long enough to record some usable data. Again, the ocean triumphed over man made science! The recorded data had been compromised and could not be taken as reliable, because a fish about 8 inches long was found trapped inside the wire mesh cage. Apparently, when the fish was tiny, it used the instrument housing as a habitat to escape predators and one day found itself too large to get out through the small wire mesh squares.

On the last dive of that day, Jim Washburn and I were teamed up and our mission was to search for the last lost instrument. Our search proved unsuccessful, so we terminated the dive and started our ascent to the decompression station. Our dive depth had reached 150 feet and we were obligated to stop at 20 feet and at 10 feet for decompression. As we ascended to 60 feet, I was facing Jim who was even with me on the ascending line, when over his shoulder in the distance I saw a large dark shape. It was at our same depth and it was coming toward us. The shape came into focus and the hair on the back of my neck stood up under my wet suit hood, it was "Jaws" headed right for us! No one had seen it during the last seven dives and I was beginning to wonder if the big shark had been waiting for me? How could I be so lucky!?

Now Jim Washburn was the proverbial "Iceman" when it came to sharks. On one dive, he and I were surrounded by three large oceanic white tips that kept circling us while we were on the decompression stop. I was a little nervous about them, but Jim seemed oblivious to their presence. About 1 minute into our seven-minute stop time he grabbed the underwater writing slate which was provided at the stop and drew a tic-tac-toe grid on it with a grease pencil. He then marked an X in one of the squares and handed it to me.

It seemed bizarre to me that we would play tic-tac-toe with three large man-eating type sharks circling us, but what the heck; if they decided to attack, there was little we could do about it, so Jim and I just played tic-tac-toe with the big sharks marauding about us. It was strange that the tic-tac-toe episode would enter my mind as a shark that could eat all those white tips for breakfast was coming directly at us in 60 feet of water, but then, my mind was always given to creating macabre humor.

The monster shark was only about 40 yards from us and I instinctively switched to self-defense mode! I stopped ascending and Jim looked at me, his eyes quizzing me for the reason we had stopped. The shark was now within 25 yards and I reached down and pulled the diving knife out of the scabbard tied to my leg as if it would do any good against this monster fish, but at least it was something and at that time it was all I had!

Jim had his back to the great white and I grabbed his arm and spun him around in front of me. Now he was staring at a really,

really big shark coming right at us with its' huge mouth open brandishing a large array of sharp teeth! The impact of seeing that big shark coming at us immediately got the "ice man's" attention and with me directly behind him, he propelled us both backward, about 10 yards away from the approaching shark.

I had no idea what to do next except to engage in an underwater battle that I was probably going to lose! I made up my mind right then that if I was going to eaten by this shark, it would be the most painful meal it ever had! Jim was still fining us backwards when the big shark turned sharply away and headed down into deeper water. "Oh thank God!" I mumbled into my regulator. Jim and I wasted no time resuming our ascent to the decompression station and I can't say that adherence to our proper rate of ascent was a priority.

As we arrived at the decompression stop, I signaled up to our safety diver. He could see that I had my knife drawn, and I gave him the hand sign for big shark. As soon as he realized what I was telling him, he began to do a nervous 360° scan of the surrounding water. Now Jim and I were faced with a dilemma. Go to the surface and probably get the bends, or try to decompress and possibly get eaten!
Jim grabbed the underwater slate and quickly wrote "go? or stay?" I took the slate and wrote back- "stay, if we see it, we'll go!" Jim nodded and we started scanning for the shark as we waited out our two minutes at the stop depth. We now needed to ascend to the 10 foot stop for 7 minutes.

As we waited through the seven minutes which seemed like forever, I formulated a plan. If the shark came back, we would abandon the decompression and try to make it into the Zodiac then run for the ship an attempt to solve the potential bends problem with surface decompression in the chamber. Finally, the stop time was up and there was no sign of the shark. Jim and I needed no assistance in getting into the Zodiac still wearing our heavy gear!

Once back aboard the ship we counted our blessings. Jim and I discussed our encounter with the team and within earshot of several of the coast guard deck crew. Most of them had seen the great shark's huge fin cruising around the surface over the past two days. After Jim and I had finished our story and our team went back to their duties, one of the deck crew came up to Jim and I and said in a low voice, "I admire you guys, but you have to be crazy as hell to go diving with that monster out there!" Jim and I looked at each other and simultaneously looked at the crewmen and nodded in agreement! We then dressed out of our suits and went to the ward room to plan the next day's "crazy as hell dives!"

The rest of the diving team set about recycling our gear and scheduling teams for the next few days of diving. Vince told me that since I seem to attract the great white shark on my dives, he had trouble getting anyone to volunteer to dive with me, so he volunteered himself. I told Vince that I couldn't guarantee that we would see it again on our dives and he quickly assured me that that would be fine with him!

The Sea Use III mission ended on a very successful note. We accomplished all our planned tasks, recovered all the instruments from the previous year's mission and no one was eaten by the Great White Shark.

DRAWING OF DIVERS WORKING ON THE 1800 FOOT CHAIN HIGHWAY THAT RUNS EAST TO WEST ACROSS THE TOP OF THE PINNACLE. THE SHIP IS MOORED TO ONE OF THE ROCK BOLT ANCHORS

ONE OF THE THREE ROCK BOLT ANCHORS IMPLANTED ON THE PINNACLE OF COBB SEAMOUNT

VINCE AND ME WITH DAMAGED SCIENTIFIC EQUIPMENT THAT WAS RECOVERED ON THE SEA USE II MISSION

CHAPTER 32
MORE MISSIONS TO COBB

Over the next 4 years there were four more missions to the Cobb Seamount. Sea Use III-C was a two-ship operation with the Coast Guard Cutter Cactus and the FS-313 coastal freighter operated by the Army National Guard. The Sea Use diving team sailed aboard the Cactus, again captained by Commander Boyce. The Cactus departed about four days before the Army ship. Our mission was to lay 1800feet of battleship anchor chain across the pinnacle of the seamount to serve as an underwater "chain highway" for diver orientation and scientific equipment location.

We also would prepare a temporary mooring for the Army ship and assist with installing three permanent anchors along the "chain highway". The Army ship was bringing out a group of commercial divers from Ocean Systems Corp. They had won a contract to drill three coring holes, retrieve the cores for scientific study and insert rock-bolt anchors into each hole. The anchor bolts were about five feet long and would be cemented into the cored holes. the anchor bolts would provide a steel pad eye and a large shackle for permanently anchoring ships at the seamount during future missions.

Both the Cactus and the FS-313 would be on the seamount for two days while the Army ship was assisted by Sea Use divers in accomplishing a mooring, so Ocean Systems could start drilling operations. After the mooring operation, most of the Sea Use divers returned to Astoria with the Cactus. Six of our most experienced divers and I transferred to the FS-313 to support the rest of the Sea Use III-C mission.

When we left the Cobb Seamount that year, we had established an undersea highway stretching 1800 feet across the pinnacle with station markers every 100 feet from stations zero in the middle to 900 feet east and 900 feet west. We had three rock-bolt anchors that were sufficient to hold a ship at anchor on the pinnacle of the undersea mountain. From the core samples taken, from the drilled holes the scientists could determine important information about the earth's magnetic field.

The Sea Use IV mission was with the Coast Guard, but this time we had a different skipper and a new Chief Bosun Mate. Chief Russ Homewood. Fortunately, Chief Mac had briefed the new Chief about the diving team and his working with Vince.

Chief Homewood and Vince hit it off right from the start and became fast friends during the mission. On Sea Use IV, we utilized the rock-bolt anchors and developed an open ocean diver assisted mooring technique that proved to be very effective. We explored the chain highway and verified that all the station markers were still in place. It was on this mission that we placed the seamount highway sign. At zero station, we secured a highway crossroads sign. On one side, it read Cactus Avenue and Aquanaut Street and on the other side an arrow points east and reads, Astoria 270 miles. On the opposite side an arrow points west and reads Japan 2468 miles. I doubt that any wayfaring undersea traveler will ever use it for directions, but just the idea that it's out there is both humorous and gratifying to us Sea Use divers.

On this mission, we also came prepared for "JAWS" and on all the dives we cared an M-16 Bang Stick, which fired an M-16 projectile if impacted on a shark. We were not sure whether the Bang Stick would drive the great white shark off, or just make it mad! We also brought a shark cage with us to do a night study of shark activity below the surface around the ship. "Murphy's Law" prevailed, and just because we were prepared to study and photograph shark activity on the mission, virtually none were observed and there was no sign of "JAWS."

CHAPTER 33
BELIEVE IT OR NOT

A last mission project was to secure a wave meter to the mountain top by anchoring it to one of the rock-bolt anchors and the chain highway. Bill Aggenbach was my teammate on this dive. Bill was an excellent diver and one of my assistant diving instructors in the community college Scientific and Engineering Diving Program. Bill was also one of our technical specialists on the Sea Use missions. Our project was to position and anchor the Advanced Research Project Agency (ARPA) Wave Meter. The instrument was designed to measure wave heights across the pinnacle of the mountain during the winter and spring storms.

The area we had chosen to anchor the instrument was located within 20 feet of the chain highway and one of the three rock-bolt anchors. The instrument was housed in a cylinder about 2 feet in diameter and about 3 feet high. It was surrounded by a protective structure of steel bars in the shape of a pyramid. It was tightly sealed and had no wire cages or Styrofoam balls. It was snapper proof! We planned to attach one corner of the base structure to the rock-bolt and the other two corners to the chain highway.

Bill and I had reached the area for the installation and checked the depth at 130 feet. We signaled the Zodiac crew to have the ship lower the instrument. The deck crew had secured a raft of large Styrofoam blocks to the top of the instrument to provide some buoyancy. The instrument would be heavy enough to sink, but light enough due to the lift of the Styrofoam so that Bill and I would be able to move into its' final position once it was on the bottom.

As soon as the instrument was on the bottom, Bill and I moved it into position and started securing the instrument to the rock-bolt anchor and chain highway. With our limited bottom time, we didn't have any time to waste. We used some strong chain lengths to secure the wave meter to the chain highway and secure the other end to the rock-bolt anchor. We used steel turnbuckles to snug the instrument to the bottom.

During the securing process, we attracted several large Red Snapper and rock fish. Some of them were more than two feet long and weighed 25 to 30 pounds. I was now busy tightening up the turnbuckles when the huge, ugly face of a rock fish filled the oval window of my mask. I tried to look around it, but every time I moved my head, the fish would move with me and totally block my vision with its' large body. I tried to continue working by Braille and was doing a fair job of it until Mr. fish, decided that the shiny metal retainer ring around my mask was something to eat and began to bite and pull at my mask.

I tried to ignore the fish's efforts to remove my mask and continue working, but this damned fish was determined to eat my mask! Finally, it succeeded in dislodging the mask from my face. Water flooded in and covered my nose and eyes. Now I had to stop and push away the big fish and clear my mask of water. When the mask cleared and I could see again, there was my finny nemesis blocking my vision and eyeing my mask for another try.

This was getting ridiculous and I was getting fed up with this stupid fish. I took a good swipe at it with the big Crescent Wrench I was using to tighten the turnbuckles. I missed! The fish swam in a large circle and came right back! I took another swipe at it and this time it swam away. Now I noticed that Bill had stopped his work and had been taking in the spectacle. I could tell by his bubble pattern that he was laughing and I flashed Bill a hand sign not exclusively used for underwater.

It was during my communication with Bill that Mr. fish sought his revenge for the Crescent Wrench whipping. Suddenly it dove from somewhere above me, chomped on to my mask and started to pull it off my head. I conked the big fish with the wrench. It let go of my mask, but not until it was loose from my face and floating away in the current. Now, it is not cool to lose your diving mask and have your vision go fuzzy 130 feet underwater on the top of a mountain 270 miles in the middle of an ocean. In reaction, I dropped the wrench and went after my mask with both hands.

I recovered the mask with a couple of fin kicks and had replaced it and purged it of water. I got clear vision just in time to see my dropped wrench go sailing past me in the mouth of a huge red snapper. Oh, great! This fish was hauling off with the only tool we had to finish the task and we didn't have much time left! I was amazed that it could carry the heavy wrench, but it didn't seem to be having any trouble at all!

Instinctively, I struck out after the fish and my wrench. When the snapper realized that I was giving chase, it sped up and I was getting way behind and burning up too much air! I was just about to give up the chase when the snapper must have decided what it had was not good to eat, and it dropped the wrench. By the time I retrieved it, I could barely see the wave instrument in the distance.

As a good diving buddy, Bill had followed me on my wild snapper chase. He was only a few yards behind me trying to keep his laughter from drowning him! Holding the wrench up for Bill to see and trying to slow my breathing from the chase, I got caught up in the humor and started laughing too. I could imagine what a ribbing I would get from the team when I tell them that a fish pulled off my mask and stole my wrench, and that's why we couldn't finish the task.

Suddenly, reality hit me. I looked at my bottom timer. "Holy Snapper," seems more appropriate than "mackerel." We had only 10 minutes left on our dive time. I looked at my depth gauge and fortunately the chase had not led us into deeper water and we were still at 130 feet. I motioned to Bill and signaled the urgency of getting to the instrument and try to finish the task before having to ascend. We beat a hasty retreat to our work area and I quickly tightened all the turnbuckles, while Bill kept big fish from trying to eat our equipment. Once Bill and I were on the decompression stop, the full humor of the situation hit us again and our regulator exhausts poured laughter bubbles into the ocean. We were still laughing when we got into the Zodiac!

THESE HUGE FISH ARE ALWAYS ARPUND THE DIVERS TRYING TO ATTACK THE DIVERS GEAR OR MASK OR TOOLS.

DIVER PETTING THE BACK OF ONE OF THE BIG FISH. THEY DON'T SEEM TO BE AFAID OF CONTACT WITH THE DIVERS

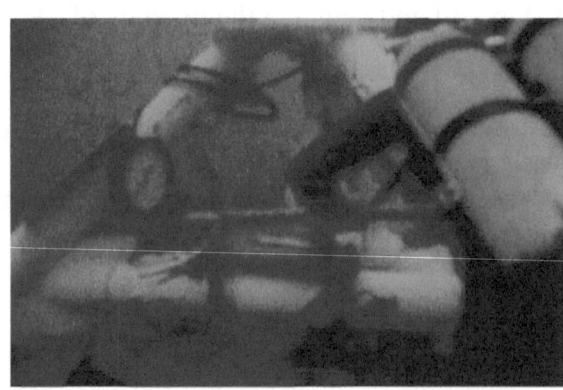

DIVER WITH ONE OF THE PIECES OF EQUIPMENT USED TO TEST THE STRENGTH OF THE ROCK BOLT ANCHOR. THE BIG FISH ARE ALWAYS WAITING TO INTERFERE WITH THE DIVER'S WORK.

CHAPTER 34
THE PAIN DIVE

There were three more missions to Cobb Seamount. Sea Use VI was with the U.S. navy research ship "**Bartlett**". On this ten day mission, we anchored the ship and placed a large acoustic sound transmitter on the eastern end of the pinnacle in 160 feet of water. There were lots of sharks on this mission! More than I had seen at any other time on the seamount. On any given dive, there were as many as 30 to 40 large pelagic sharks milling around near the surface. They were all large sharks, some Bulls, Duskys, Silkies and Blues, but this time, no Great White sharks!

On Sea Use VI and VII, we did mostly scientific and photographic tasks. On the last mission, Sea Use VIII, we performed an experimental dive to 160 feet for 10 minutes and ascended to the surface with no decompression. The same dive profile was conducted in the chamber at the Institute of Applied Physiology and Medicine in Seattle. All the experimental subjects for these dives were volunteers from the "Sea Use" dive team.

New equipment for detecting bubbles in the blood was used during the chamber dives, and although some bubbles were detected in three of the experimental divers, no one developed any symptoms of decompression sickness. Duplication of the diving schedule in the open ocean resulted in a greater quantity of bubbles in most divers and I was stricken with severe pain in my right elbow. The Doppler Detection Monitor recorded many bubbles in the blood returning to my heart from my lower body. In other words, I got the "*bends*!"

The reason for the experiment was to compare the old navy decompression table dive schedule in the chamber to the same schedule on an open ocean dive to see if ocean dives, being more stressful, contribute to the development of bubbles causing the bends. Since the Doppler method was new technology, we could measure the difference in bubble quantity and propensity to cause the Bends.

Since we suspected that the ocean dives might create more potential bends, we were well prepared for the situation. We had a full sized two lock decompression chamber aboard the ship. We also had a Submarine Medical Officer, Dr. Bill Postles and five diving medical technicians to assist Dr. Postles with any required treatments. We had two women on the team, Sandy Olerich was an R.N. trained in submarine medicine, and Sharon Dodge was a qualified Sea Use diver and one of our submarine medical technicians.

Now, I don't want to end our stories of the Sea Use missions with me getting the bends, but this story has a twist! I had just gotten onto the deck of the ship from my experimental dive and was taking off my wet suit jacket, when I started feeling pressure and pain in my right elbow. It was a burning sensation as if someone were pouring hot lead into the joint. As soon as I reported the symptoms, Dr. Postles checked me with the Doppler monitor and detected a large amount of bubbles in the blood leading to my heart.

The Dr. quickly administered some medications designed to help minimize physical damage and assist in the recompression treatment. Now it was time to get into the recompression chamber and start recompression treatment! This consisted of compressing my body to a simulated depth of 60 feet of sea water and then gradually reducing the pressure as the nitrogen gas bubbles dissipate without causing any serious damage. We were also employing an experimental treatment protocol using oxygen and medication.

Dr. Postles and I quickly entered the main compartment of the chamber and pulled the hatch shut. Immediately, our chamber operator, John Eriksen, opened the valve and began pressurizing the chamber compartment to a simulated depth of 60 feet. Dr. Postles and I began compensating for the pressure by holding our nose and blowing gently to equalize the pressure in our ears. The rapid compression made the air warm. When the roar of blowing, compressed air stopped, and a fresh flow of cool air was started to match a release of air from the chamber compartment. This would ventilate the chamber while keeping the pressure constant, and in addition to providing a fresh flow of air it would keep unwanted excess carbon dioxide at a safe level.

The main lock of the chamber was about 6 feet in diameter and about 8 feet long. Dr. Postles and I were seated on a metal bench directly below one of the five viewing ports made of clear, thick Lexan, a clear, strong plastic material. These ports allow the technicians to observe the condition of the personnel inside the chamber.

Relaxing a bit from the pain in my right elbow, I eased back on the bench and stretched out my legs that were still clad in my neoprene wet suit. In a hurry to begin treatment, there was no opportunity to remove all my gear. As I stared at my outstretched right leg, I was shocked by what I saw! Still attached to my leg, was my diving knife and attached to the knife scabbard was the day night flare cartridge that all of us divers wore to be used as a signal in the event we became separated from the Zodiac boat and the ship and lost in the sea.

The reason for my semi-panic reaction was that the enriched oxygen environment of the chamber under pressure was no place for a pyrotechnic device! If for any reason the flare were to ignite, everything in the chamber that could burn, including our bodies, would incinerate with the heat of a blast furnace! For a second, I had a vision of barbecued diver in a wreath of bright orange smoke!

Immediately, I called out to John over the intercom. "John, pressurize the outer transfer lock to our depth now!!" there was a moment of silence. "What's the problem?" John replied. "look at my right leg John!" I said as I held it up toward the port. John's response of "oh my god!" was partly obscured by the clanging of the outer lock a hatch followed by the whoosh of pressurizing air. In a moment, the hatch between the main lock and the outer transfer lock popped open and in less than a micro-second, I had put my knife and its deadly package onto the outer lock, closed the hatch and called for John to return the transfer lock to the outside pressure.

I don't think Dr. Postles was fully aware of the situation until the flare was safely on the way to sea level pressure in the outer lock. In our haste to get treatment started, we inadvertently set ourselves up for a potentially tragic accident. The full realization of how an urgent situation can cause normally careful professionals to overlook an obvious danger was sobering, and Dr. Postles and I breathed a sigh of relief! The experimental recompression schedule was successful and 3 hours later, I emerged from the chamber pain free with no residual effects.

The results of the seamount exploration eliminated the feasibility of putting an undersea station on the pinnacle of Cobb Seamount. It did show that the seamount produced extremely unusual sea conditions over the pinnacle and that large ships like Oil tankers must avoid the area when storm seas exist. We also learned that installing measuring devises on the pinnacle will require equipment designed to withstand the tremendous force of a disturbed ocean!

Our exploration of the seamount was a great adventure and I have to quote from the exploration of Lewis and Clark "It was not what we went to find that was as important as what we did find!"

TWO COMPARTMENT DECOMPRESSION CHAMBER BEING LOADED ABOARD THE COAST GUARD CUTTER FOR A MISSION TO THE COBB SEAMOUNT

DECOMPRESSION CHAMBER READY FOR OPERATIONS AT THE COBB SEAMOUNT

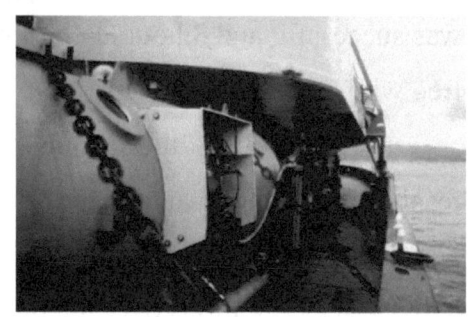

SMALL COAST GUARD CERTIFIED DECOMPRESSION CHAMBER USED ON MOST OF THE SEA USE MISSIONS. THIS CHAMBER IS 9 FEET LONG AND 36 INCHES INTERNAL DIAMETER

DECOMPRESSION TREATMENT TIMES CAN BE 18 HOURS OR MORE. SEA USE DIVERS CAN NOT BE CLAUSTROPHOBIC!

CHAPTER 35
IS THIS THE END?

I was 40 years old when we completed the Sea Use missions in 1975, and those missions along with my long river swim were the great adventures of my life! During the next few years, I would dedicate myself to teaching young men and women to become professional divers. I left my position at Bellevue community college to work with Maurice Talbot, Director of the Undersea Technician Program at Highline Community College. This was a two year AAS degree program, which prepared young men and women for a career in commercial diving.

During the five years following the Sea Use missions, our family life was marred by tragedy. Susan's diabetes caused kidney failure and she was placed on the kidney dialysis machine. We elected to do home dialysis, and for the next four years I would become Susan's primary care giver and dialysis technician. During those four years, she would receive a kidney donated by her brother John Craig, who accompanied me on my 557-mile river swim.

That kidney functioned for about six months and then unfortunately, it failed. Susan received another kidney from an organ donor about six months later. It failed after only four months. Another six months of home dialysis, and the damage to her system was too much! She went to the hospital in April and passed away on April 17, 1977. Our son Ron was in his first year of high school and

Scott was in his last year of middle school. I think the toughest thing I ever had to do in my life, was on the morning of Susan's passing, when I woke up my two young sons to tell them that their mother was gone.

Her passing was hard on them; but they both knew how much suffering she had endured after the kidneys had failed. The boys and I were very close after their mother left us. They were both active in junior high school and high school sports, and I will always have a residual callous on my rear from those wooden bleachers while watching their games. Both Ron and Scott were wonderful sons who I knew would grow up to be fine men.

I was now 42 years old with two sons in high school. I was a tenured faculty member of a local community college, teaching in the Undersea Technician Program. I was happy and content with my life. I enjoyed teaching young men and women to use their commercial diving skills in the industry. We had a very successful diving program at Highline, and I thoroughly enjoyed working with Maurice Talbot and teaching. Someone, introducing me for an award one time said I had a teaching gene. Maybe they were right, as I do love to teach. Well, you might think that I would now coast into retirement as a vocational college teacher. One would think that I had lived enough adventures by now, and that I would be content to do middle age things. Not so! Life had other plans for me; but as Paul Harvey would say, *"That is the rest of the story!"*

THE END

Made in United States
Troutdale, OR
02/26/2024